The English Critic

From Chaucer to Auden

N. L. Clay

Published by

ATLANTIC

PUBLISHERS & DISTRIBUTORS (P) LTD

7/22, Ansari Road, Darya Ganj, New Delhi-110002
Phones: +91-11-40775252, 40775214, 23273880, 23275880
Fax: +91-11-23285873
Web: www.atlanticbooks.com
E-mail: orders@atlanticbooks.com

Disclaimer

- The author and the publisher have taken every effort to the maximum of their skill, expertise and knowledge to provide correct material in the book. Even then if some mistakes persist in the content of the book, the publisher does not take responsibility for the same. The publisher shall have no liability to any person or entity with respect to any loss or damage caused, or alleged to have been caused directly or indirectly, by the information contained in this book.
- The author has fully tried to follow the copyright law. However, if any work is found to be similar, it is unintentional and the same should not be used as defamatory or to file legal suit against the author.
- If the readers find any mistakes, we shall be grateful to them for pointing out those to us so that these can be corrected in the next edition.
- All disputes are subject to the jurisdiction of Delhi courts only.

Printed & bound in India by Atlantic Print Services

Preface

In compiling this volume the Editor has kept before him the needs of Sixth Forms in Secondary Schools and of classes in Training Colleges and Universities. For them the need is of an introduction to Criticism which will awaken and sustain interest in the art, which will provide a good basis for the serious study of literature, and which can be read with enjoyment by those who know but little of the history of literature.

In choosing extracts, the Editor has interpreted "Critic" as "one who has made a valuable contribution to criticism" rather than "one who has made a profession of criticism." Consequently, writers are included who may have achieved eminence in other spheres. Similarly, the Editor at times feels that he might offer apologies to those well-known critics, who had to be excluded for reasons of space.

Very often a critical passage of major importance is not easily accessible, because it is concealed in a lengthy work. The present volume rescues such passages from semi-oblivion. The extracts are limited so as to contain the essential core of the writer's argument, while the introductions give sufficient information to enable the reader to start suitably prepared. This obviates the danger of paraphrasing an author's theory, a regrettable practice to which necessity sometimes drives harassed teachers. Occasionally, the Editor offers a series of linked extracts, which preserve the continuity of the writer's ideas by omitting irrelevant matter.

While *The English Critic* renders important passages easy of access, it is definitely a book for study rather than for reading. The varied questions are meant to stimulate the student to think about the ideas he has read, and to prevent him from swallowing them whole. Some questions are sufficiently hard to test the keenest student.

Many thanks are due to Mr. A. J. W. Hill and to Mr. R. Welldon Finn, as members of my publishers, for their unfailing help and guidance, and particularly for enabling me to include such a generous share of contemporary criticism. Thanks, too, are owed to all who have helped to read the proofs, and to the following for their permission to print copyright material: the Executors of the late Mrs. F. E. Hardy for Thomas Hardy's "The Science of Fiction"; Mrs. Galsworthy, the Author's Literary Executor, for an extract from a letter by John Galsworthy contained in H. V. Marrot's *Life and Letters of John Galsworthy* (Heinemann); Messrs. 'Faber and Faber' for "The Metaphysical Poets" from T. S. Eliot's *Selected Essays*; Messrs. Jonathan Cape for part of W. H. Auden's Preface to *Selected Poems of Robert Frost*; and Mr. Herbert Read for "The Poetry of Gerard Manley Hopkins" from *In Defence of Shelley, and Other Essays* (Heinemann).

—N. L. Clay

Contents

Introduction

I

To the ordinary man of to-day "Critic" seems to mean "one who delivers judgment in print."

It is not so much that the ordinary man does not rely on his own judgment as that he has excessive reverence for the printed verdict of the professional. He will argue fiercely with the man next to him in the football ground but will change his mind about the quality of a broadcast item after reading in his morning paper what the Radio Critic says. He takes the Dramatic Critic's word when deciding what play to see and makes his book-lists from the selection of compliments bestowed by critics and artfully displayed by advertisers.

Many who take their reading seriously smile with superiority at this respect for printed opinion, but fail to see how little they themselves rely on their own opinions. Success in public examinations has often been the reward of those who have neither convictions nor courage but who can reproduce the judgments of others. Even when discussing books in friendly talk they frequently parrot the findings of critics. This weakness on the part of the reader tends to make the reviewers of our newspapers and journals proud of their following and influence, arrogant towards readers and condescending towards authors.

Many disreputable features of present-day reviewing would disappear if the common reader was more self-reliant. But he must be able to rely on something more solid than whim or fancy: he needs some knowledge of critical principles as a basis for judging and developing his own power of judgment. The more he is familiar with the great critics of the past, the less he will think of the little ones of to-day. Indeed, unless he has that familiarity, he cannot fully understand or benefit from the great critics of to-day. For when they discuss seemingly modern problems (which have in fact so often been topics for critics of previous centuries) they are building on the foundations made by their predecessors. "Is verse the right medium for drama?" "When is a happy ending wrong?" "Why is 'escape-literature' popular?"—Jonson, Dryden, Steele gave their opinions years ago: it is foolish to discard or ignore what they said, though we may flatter ourselves that we can bring it up to date. As Chesterton says, "Real development is not leaving things behind, as on a road, but drawing life from them, as from a root."

II

Criticism (like religion) is an ideal. It is something difficult to achieve but worth attempting. Criticism is more than judgment-passing just as religion is more than church-going. Few are qualified to come within grasp of the ideal, but those few, the Wesleys or the Booths, the Coleridges or Eliots, give to others vision and inspiration.

Some periods of time seem to favour the pursuit of the ideal more than others. In the Age of Elizabeth the critic has no accepted body of work on which to base his standards, but must attempt to judge the work of his own country by the standards of classical literature. In the seventeenth century the charge that what England is writing is inferior to the literature of France seems to be an obstacle, yet Dryden almost surmounts it. "With Dryden we are wandering in search of Truth; whom we find, if we find her at all, dressed in the graces of elegance; and if we miss her, the labour of the pursuit rewards itself; we are led only through fragrance and flowers," says Dr. Johnson. Dryden did more than mingle delight with instruction: in upholding "English methods for English minds and English matter" he was the first great English critic. He set a noble example to those who asked of a writer not "What is his work worth?" but "What is his religion?" and "What is his politics?"

In the eighteenth century the spirit of the time encourages if it does not insist on Conformity. To be correct is the essential thing, to conform to the rules established by the Classics, by Reason, by Good Sense. Even at the end of the century Reynolds preaches to art students "an implicit obedience to the rules of art, as established on the practice of the great masters, perfect and infallible guides." Orthodoxy is supreme, "enthusiasm" is suspect. In such an age it is a bold critic, who dares praise experiments that do not square with the accepted rules.

In the first half of the nineteenth century politics are an obstacle to true criticism. *The Edinburgh Review, The Quarterly, Blackwood's* open their columns to critics, but they are often guilty of judging a writer not on his merits but on his politics. They begin the practice of tempting writers to desert creative work for reviewing (at twenty guineas a page). Jeffrey, greater than the rest and sounder, creates an audience for criticism (over twelve thousand copies cf one issue were frequently sold). Macaulay shows that the reading of criticism can be enjoyable, even exciting. Arnold's fulminations against the tendency to be satisfied with the second-rate help to create higher standards. Carlyle attacks parochialism, insisting that in judging the poets of our own land we must consider aspects of poetry which are revealed in German literature. The pursuit may be harder, but the ideal is nearer when we can build on the literature of Russia, Scandinavia and America as well as on our own.

The twentieth century brings to the front an old problem, the choice between "two paths, constructive acceptance (the road of the builders) and the way of revolt (the road of the adventurers and pioneers)" as Mr. J. L. Lowes puts it. The demand for reading-matter to enable the ordinary man and his wife to occupy their leisure has led to the present huge output of books, the many ways of choosing books for the bewildered reader, the increase in the quantity of reviewing, and in the rarity of valuable criticism at a time when it is most needed.

III

What makes an ideal Critic? "The best critics," says Mr. Clutton Brock, "are those who, having freed their minds from wrong suggestions, are therefore able to experience works of art." Is this an advance on the eighteenth-century writer who confesses, "I love to give my judgment, such as it is, from my immediate perceptions, without much fatigue of thinking"? This theory which attributes to the mind the qualities of a sensitized plate, and which limits criticism to "the adventures of a soul among masterpieces," with its suggestion that one person's sensations are more important than the work of art, is too unscientific for to-day.

Spingarn, in 1911, said that the critic should ask and answer honestly these questions:

What has the author tried to do?

How has he fulfilled his intention?

What is he striving to express?

How has he expressed it?

What impression does his work make on me?

How can I best express that impression?

Notice that "the personal response" instead of being the only question, is the fifth of a series of six. Such an orderly procedure has been popularized by Croce, and is accepted to-day as a perfectly sound guide.

Mr. Middleton Murry, in *A Critical Credo,* offers a comparable method.

"First, the critic should endeavour to convey the whole effect of the work he is criticising, its peculiar uniqueness. Second, to work back and define the unique quality of the sensibility which necessitated this expression. Third, to establish the determining causes of this sensibility. (Here the relevant circumstances of the writer's life have their proper place.) Fourth, to analyse the means by which this sensibility was given expression, in other words to conduct a technical examination into the style. Fifth, a still closer examination of a perfectly characteristic passage, that is, a passage in which the author's sensibility is completely expressed. This fifth and final movement is really a return to the first, but with the important difference that the relevant material has been ordered and placed before the reader."

But there is a much wider conception of "critic" than "one who passes judgment on one poem or one piece of creative work." We often need to test the soundness of a criticism of the whole work of one writer, or of the work of an age. Then we can ask if the critic possesses the right attitude, for "the best criticism is valuable not so much for its particular judgments as for its attitude." Mr. Lynd would reject anyone who is merely "an inspector of literary weights and measures," Mr. Priestley anyone who betrays" the weary gesture that directs the author and his work to their appointed pigeon-hole." The critic should feel that Literature is not an institution but a living force, something of value to people to-day. His purpose should be not to exalt himself at the expense of the writer but to enlarge the understanding and sharpen the faculties of the reader.

The critic must have both interest and knowledge: he must be absorbed in the present problems of literature and must be able "to bring the forces of the past to bear upon the solution of these problems." Although mere learning, even the most capacious memory, is not enough, yet the solidity that may make the literary historian uninspiring will, if accompanied by other essential qualities, prevent inconsistency or injustice. The expert in one period may reveal distressing ignorance of another. The ideal critic should be sound on all periods and unassailable in the one period that is most to his own taste. Expert knowledge of one period will have brought home to him the importance of the social forces that produce and shape the work of a writer.

The critic's tools, comparison and analysis, are insufficient without taste, a delicate sensitiveness corresponding to the fine palate of the tea-taster. (Unfortunately, fineness of taste, besides being rare, is too often unable to sustain its high standard over a long period of testing.) Taste needs honesty and courage to support it, for we ask that the critic should record his findings without considering current fashion, and, no matter how eminent the author he is studying, should perceive and point out where a work changes from "great" to "good."

A critic needs *gusto.* He should be able to communicate his own delight and interest; his keenness should be infectious. We ask him to share his enthusiasms, and even his dislikes. The reader should be able to derive pleasure from the way in which the critic expresses himself. The more the critic is an artist in prose, the more we shall turn to his pages with delight. Mr. Somerset Maugham's three touchstones of good prose—simplicity, lucidity, and euphony—can be applied to criticism above all other literary forms.

We ask much: matter of value as the body of criticism, clearness and precision to give light and strength to the body, enthusiasm to add warmth, and individuality to unite them and communicate flavour. Others demand more. Mr. Day Lewis tells us — "There can be only two valuable kinds of criticism. The first aims simply to erect signposts for the reader, to help him over difficult places, and to make him feel that the journey is worth undertaking. The second, creative criticism is rare as any other form of creative writing. Where the critic has studied an author, lived with him in the spirit for a long space of time, become saturated with him, an affinity may grow up between them, so that some of the original power of the master is transmitted to the disciple." Alice Meynell supplies a personal demand at the end of her list of the qualities she looks for: "precision, and its rare companions—liberty, flight, height, courage, a sense of space, and a sense of closeness, readiness for spiritual experience, and all the gravity, all the resolution of the lonely reader."

Recently, our attention has been directed to the social implications of literature. Mr. Herbert Read has declared that the only basic literary criticism is that "which traces the origins of the work of art in the psychology of the individual and in the economic structure of the society." This is an elaboration of the belief that literature is a real part of the life of the people. Such criticism is seen in its extreme form in a recent attempt to tell the story of English Literature from the point of view of the society. Here the danger lies in attempting to fit writers into an arbitrarily constructed framework, and so passing over that part of their work which is independent of the social forces of the time. It is, however, a useful reminder that the critic must not in his attempt to trace the growth of such a form as the novel forget that literature has always been dependent on human needs.

We may never find the ideal critic: we may never even agree on what makes an ideal critic. But there should be no disagreement about our debt to the critic or about the importance of his work. We who appreciate that debt should defend him against such attacks as Chekov's — "Critics are like horseflies which prevent the horse from ploughing" or that of Sibelius — "Remember, a statue has never been set up in honour of a critic." The English Critic needs no statues: he does not lack readers and their gratitude is warm and living.

1

Chaucer

Geoffrey Chaucer (1340 (?)–1400), often called "our first great modern writer," seems nearer to us of the twentieth century than many writers who were born long after him. His widespread activities brought him into contact with "all sorts and conditions of men": his art enabled him to use his experience so that his characters are true of all time. To him we owe the five-footed iambic line of verse, for so long and in so many ways the backbone of English poetry. He took a dialect, ennobled it by using it for immortal matter, and helped it to become a language. "The first great literary artist of his country"—a Frenchman's compliment—hc looks on his fellows with interest and sympathy and thinks of his craft as one that is serious and important.

In *The Canterbury Tales* (*c.* 1385) he describes lovingly and faithfully a band of pilgrims, and sets them off to Canterbury under a worthy Host, who demands tales from each pilgrim. The Monk, when his turn comes, is asked for something merry and offers one of his many "Tragedies." The first extract gives the Monk's idea of tragedy, the second adds the Plain Man's attitude to "uplift" or instruction without the sugar-coating of amusement.

A mark (') over a vowel indicates that it is to be sounded as a separate syllable.

From The Canterbury Tales

(*a*)

[The Monk is speaking]

"Tragédie is to seyn a certeyn storie,
As oldé bookes maken us memorie,
Of hym that stood in greet prosperitee,
And is y-fallen out of heigh degree
Into myserie, and endèth wrecchedly;
And they ben versified communely,
Of six feet, which men clepen exametron.
In prose eek been endited[1] many oon
And eek in metre in many a sondry wysè."

(*b*)

[The pilgrims, after enduring seventeen such tragedies, speak their mind.]

"Hoo!" quod the Knyght, "good sire, namoore of this!
That ye han seyd is right ynough, y-wis,
And muchel moore; for litel hevynessè
Is right ynough to muchè folk, I gessè
I seye for me it is a gret disesè
Where as men han been in gret welthe and esè,
To heeren of hire sodeyn fal, alias!
And the contrarie is joye and greet solas,
As whan a man hath ben in greet estaat,
And clymbeth up, and wexeth *[grows]* fortunat,
And there abydeth in prosperitee;
Swich thyng is gladsom, as it thynketh me,
And of swich thyng were goodly for to tellè."
"Ye," quod oure Host, "by Seintè Poulès bellè!
Ye seye right sooth; this Monk he clappeth lowdè;
He spak how 'Fortune covered with a clowdè.'
I noot never what, and als of.' tragédiè'
Right now ye herde, and, pardee! no remédiè
It is for to biwaylle, or to compleynè
That that is doon; and als, it is a peynè,
As ye han seyd, to heere of hevynessè

Sire Monk, namoore of this, so God yow blessè!
Youre tale anoyeth all this compaignyè;
Swiche talkynge is nat worth a boterflyè,
For therinne is ther no desport ne gamè."

[1] set down.

2

Sidney

Sir Philip Sidney (1554-1586), "the perfect knight,

The soldier, courtier, bard in one,"

while he lived was looked up to as the ideal Elizabethan, and by his unselfishness at the point of death became a model Englishman. He wielded a pen as gracefully as a sword. The man whom foreign universities revered as "a general Mæcenas of Learning" wrote that lovely lyric, "My true love hath my heart and I have his" and amused himself with *Arcadia* ("the earliest example of a book written throughout in standard English speech"), with its endless experiments in form and metre, which strengthened a vogue for Pastorals and provided many playwrights with plots. As a man who had solved the problem of grafting Renaissance culture on to an English stock, as a gifted poet, he was sure of a public, and what he said carried weight.

In 1579 Stephen Gosson issued *The School of Abuse.* He had been influenced by a sermon in time of plague to abandon writing plays: this pamphlet, "a pleasant invective against poets . . . players . . . and such-like caterpillars of the commonwealth," blaming writers for the sins of the age, he boldly dedicated to Sidney. The latter replied in *An Apologie for Poetrie,* disdaining to name his opponent, but answering in a dignified way the four charges against poetry — "That a man might employ his time in better ways, That it is the mother of lies, That it is the nurse of abuse, and that Plato had the sense to banish poets from the commonwealth." The result is "the first serious work of critical theory, in English," the first attempt to formulate theory, to value contemporary work by the highest standards, to speak of poetry as one of the finest things of life.

Sidney was writing just before the richest days of Elizabethan Literature. His public, trained in an age of good schools to know the classics, was ready to buy poetry. 'Spenser had published his *Shepheardes Calender,* Marlowe and his colleagues were still at the University, Shakespeare was still assimilating Life.

In these extracts from *An Apologie for Poetrie* the spelling is modernized, but not the punctuation.

From *An Apologie for Poetrie*

(*a*)

Since then Poetry is of all human learning the most ancient, and of the most fatherly antiquity, as from whence other learning's have taken their beginnings; since it is so universal that no learned nation doth despise it, nor no barbarous nation is without it; since both Roman and Greek gave divine names unto it, the one of "prophesying" [vates], the other of "making" [poet], and that indeed that name of "making" is fit for him, considering that whereas other Arts retain themselves within their subject, and receive as it were, their being from it, the Poet only bringeth his own stuff, and doth not learn a conceit out of a matter, but maketh matter for a conceit[1]; since that neither his description nor his end containeth any evil, the thing cannot be evil; since his effects be so good as to teach goodness and to delight the learners; since therein (namely in moral doctrine, the chief of all knowledge's) he doth not only far pass the Historian, but, for instructing, is well-nigh comparable to the Philosopher, and, for moving, leaves him far behind him; since the Holy Scripture (wherein there is no uncleanness) hath whole parts in it poetical, and that even our Saviour Christ vouchsafed to use the flowers of it; since that all his kinds[2] are not only in their united forms but in their severed dissections fully commendable: I think (and think I think rightly) the laurel crown appointed for triumphing captains doth worthily (of all other learning's) honour the Poet's triumph. ...

So that since the ever-praiseworthy Poesy is full of virtue-breeding delightfulness, and void of no gift that ought to be in the noble name of learning: since the blames laid against it are either false or feeble; since the cause why it is not esteemed in England is the fault of Poet-apes, not Poets; since, lastly, our tongue is most fit to honour Poesy, and to be honoured by Poesy: I conjure you all . . . even in the name of the nine Muses, no more to scorn the sacred mysteries of Poesy, no more to laugh at the name of Poets, as though they were next inheritors to Fools, no more to jest at the reverent title of a Rhymer.

(*b*)

[After lamenting that Poetry is not honoured in England, and that little really good poetry has been written since Chaucer, he examines the state of Drama.]

Our Tragedies and Comedies (not without cause cried out against), observing rules neither of honest civility nor of skillful poetry, excepting *Gorboduc*[3] (again, I, say, of those that I have seen), which notwithstanding as it is full of stately speeches and well-sounding phrases, climbing to the height of Seneca his style, and as full of notable morality, which it doth most delightfully teach, and so obtain the very end of Poesy, yet in truth it is very defectious in the circumstances, which grieveth me, because it might not remain as an exact model of all tragedies. For it is faulty both in place and time,[4] the two necessary companions of all corporal actions. For where the stage should always represent but one place, and the uttermost time pre-supposed in it should be, both by Aristotle's precept and common reason, but one day, there is both many days, and many places, inartificially [5] imagined. But if it be so in *Gorboduc,* how much more in all the rest, where you shall have Asia of the one side, and Africa of the other, and so many other under-kingdoms, that the Player, when he cometh in, must ever begin with telling where he is, or else the tale will not be conceived! Now you shall have three ladies walk to gather flowers, and then we must believe the stage to be a garden. By and by we hear news of shipwreck in the same place, and then we are to blame if we accept it not for a rock. Upon the back of that, comes out a hideous monster, with fire and smoke, and then the miserable beholders are bound to take it for a cave. While in the meantime two armies fly in, represented with four swords and bucklers, and then what hard heart will not receive it for a pitched field?

Now, of time they are much more liberal, for ordinary it is that two young princes fall in love. After many traverses, she is got with child, delivered of a fair boy; he is lost, groweth to a man, falls in love, and is ready to get another child; and all this in two hours' space: which, how absurd it is in sense, even sense may imagine, and art hath taught, and all ancient examples justified, and, at this day, the ordinary players in Italy will not err in. Yet will some bring in an example of *Eunuchus* in Terence,[6] that containeth matter of two days, yet far short of twenty years. True it is, and so was it to be played in two days, and so fitted to the time it set forth. And though Plautus[7] hath in one place done amiss, let us hit with him, and not miss with him.

But they will say, how then shall we set forth a story, which containeth both many places and many times? And do they not know that a tragedy is tied to the laws of Poesy, and not of History, not bound to follow the story, but, having liberty, either to feign a quite new matter, or to frame the history to the most tragically convenience? Again, many things may be told which cannot be showed, if they know the difference between reporting and representing. As, for example, I may speak (though I am here) of Peru, and in speech digress from that to the description of Calicut[8]; but in action I cannot represent it without Pacolet's horse[9]: and so was the manner the Ancients took, by some Nuncius[10] to recount things done in former time or other place. Lastly, if they will represent a history, they must not (as Horace saith) begin *ab ovo,*[11] but they must come to the principal point of that one action which they will represent. By example this will be best expressed. I have a story of young Polydorus,[12] delivered for safety's sake, with great riches, by his father Priamus to Polymnestor, King of Thrace, in the Trojan war time. He after some years, hearing the overthrow of Priamus, for to make the treasure his own, murdereth the child. The body of the child is taken up by Hecuba. She the same day findeth a sleight to be revenged most cruelly of the tyrant.

Where now would one of our Tragedy writers begin, but with the delivery of the child? Then should he sail over into Thrace, and so spend I know not how many years, and travel numbers of places. But where doth Euripides? Even with the finding of the body, leaving the rest to be told by the spirit of Polydorus. This need no further to be enlarged; the dullest wit may conceive it.

But besides these gross absurdities, how all their plays be neither right tragedies nor right comedies, mingling kings and clowns, not because the matter so carrieth it, but thrust in clowns by head and shoulders, to play a part in majestical matters, with neither decency nor discretion, so as neither the admiration and commiseration, nor the right scornfulness, is by their mongrel Tragi-comedy obtained. I know Apuleius[13] did somewhat so, but that is a thing recounted with space of time, not represented in one moment: and I know the Ancients have one or two examples of tragi-comedies, as Plautus hath Amphitruo. But if we mark them well, we shall find that they never, or very daintily, match hornpipes and funerals. So falleth it out that, having indeed no right Comedy, in that comical part of our Tragedy we have nothing but scurrility, unworthy of any chaste ears, or some extreme show of doltishness, indeed fit to lift up a loud laughter, and nothing else: where the whole tract of a Comedy should be full of delight, as the Tragedy should be still maintained in a well-raised admiration.

But our comedians think there is no delight without laughter; which is very wrong, for though laughter may come with delight, yet cometh it not of delight, as though delight should be the cause of laughter; but well may one thing breed both together: nay, rather in themselves they have, as it were, a kind of contrariety: for delight we scarcely do but in things that have a convenience to ourselves or to the general nature: laughter almost ever cometh of things most disproportioned to ourselves and nature. Delight hath a joy in it, either permanent or present. Laughter hath only a scornful tickling. For example, we are ravished with delight to see a fair woman, and yet we are far from being moved to laughter. We delight in good chances, we laugh at mischance's; we delight to hear the happiness of our friends, or country, at which he were worthy to be laughed at that would laugh; we shall, contrarily, laugh sometimes to find a matter quite mistaken and go down the hill against the bias, in the mouth of such men, as for the respect of them one shall be heartily sorry, yet he cannot chose but laugh; and so is rather pained than delighted with laughter. Yet deny I not but that they may well go together; for as in Alexander's picture well set out we delight without laughter, and in twenty mad antics we laugh without delight, so in Hercules, painted with his great beard and furious countenance, in woman's attire, spinning at Omphale's commandment, it breedeth both delight and laughter. For the representing of so strange a power in love procureth delight: and the scornfulness of the action stirreth laughter.

But I speak to this purpose, that all the end of the comical part be not upon such scornful matter as stirreth laughter only, but, mixed with it, that delightful teaching which is the end of Poesy. And the great fault even in that point of laughter, and forbidden plainly by Aristotle, is that they stir laughter in sinful things, which are rather execrable than ridiculous: or in miserable, which are rather to be pitied than scorned. For what is it to make folks gape at a wretched beggar, or a beggarly clown, or, against law of hospitality, to jest at strangers, because they speak no English as well as we do? . . . But I have lavished out too many words of this play matter. (I do it because, as they are excelling parts of Poesy, so there is none so much used in England, and none can be more pitifully abused), which, like an unmannerly daughter showing a bad education, causeth her mother Poesy's honesty to be called in question.

(*a*)

[1]*conceit*—idea, flight of fancy.

[2]*all his kinds*—Pastoral, Elegiac, Iambic and Satiric Poetry, Comedy, Tragedy, Lyric Poetry, Epic or Heroic Poetry.

(*b*)

[3]*Gorboduc*—a tragedy after the style of Seneca, by Sackville and Norton, first acted 1561.

[4]*faulty both in place and time.*—The first reference to the Unities in English criticism. Sidney seems to have learned about them not in the original Greek but in Latin versions, particularly Castelvetro's Commentary (1570). This is the first of a long line of writings attributing more to Aristotle than he actually said.

[5]*inartificially*—artlessly.

[6]*Terence* (195-159 B.C.)—Roman writer of comedies. His works may be read in the original and in translation (as with the other classical writers mentioned) in the Loeb series (Heinemann). Actually the action of *Eunuchus* does not extend over two days.

[7]*Plautus* (c. 254-184 B.C.).—The best-known writer of Latin comedies, which were frequently performed in Elizabethan schools.

[8]*Calicut*—Calcutta.

[9]*Pacolet's horse*—and enchanter's horse.

[10]*Nuncius*—a messenger, such as the one, who reports the death of Samson in Milton's *Samson Agonistes* (the best English work for a study of conventions of classical drama in practice).

[11]*ab ovo*—"from the egg," *i.e.,* from the first course, or from the very beginning.

[12]*a story of young Polydorus*—an outline of the plot of *Hecuba* by Euripides (480-406 B.C.), Greek writer of tragedies.

[13]*Apuleius.*—Roman author of *The Golden Ass.*

3

Ben Jonson

Ben Jonson (1573-1637), Londoner, playwright, writer of masques, critic, poet, lived to be the last of the greater Elizabethans, proud to have been a colleague, rival and friend of Shakespeare, was a man revered and admired by the writers of a new age. He deserved his epitaph—"O rare Ben Jonson." His plays now are overshadowed by those of Shakespeare, but *The Alchemist* and *Volpone* can still entertain and satisfy. English Literary Criticism is the poorer for lack of records of the wit-combats between Shakespeare and Jonson — "like a Spanish great galleon and an English man-of-war; Master Jonson, like the former, was built far higher in learning, solid, but slow in his performances; Shakespeare, with the English man-of-war, lesser in bulk, but lighter in sailing, could turn with all tides, tack about and take advantage of all winds, by the quickness of his wit and invention." This stupendous learning is evident both in his plays and in his critical notes and jottings—*Discoveries* (published 1641).

Ben Jonson stood for Truth as he saw it. If he failed to convert his contemporaries, his influence on succeeding ages has been great and important. "The Elizabethan age was a miracle, and literature cannot live long on miracles." The magnificence of his age had its dangers and absurdities, which he saw and proclaimed. There was a real danger that authority would be flung to the winds and that every fault would be thought justified by genius. "The romantic splendour and carelessness of genius were set up for examples, which mediocrity could not follow without disaster." To stem such a tide he offered precept and practice, for his plays showed that restraint and order were not obstacles to success. "Jonson was preaching decorum in an age of riot." In his *Discoveries* we can read and enjoy his high-spirited teaching, his manly vigour, and above all his good sense. This book is not written for contemporaries or for posterity: it is really a commonplace book in which he set down passages from his wide reading and comments of his own mind— "made upon men and matter as they have flowed out of his daily reading, or had their reflex to his peculiar notion of the times." But even translations emerge from the furnace of his mind in a new and highly individual mould. The first extract expounds Aristotle's principle of the Unity of Action—it is not a mere paraphrase but a re-shaping, expanding the original where necessary, with original illustrations. The second series of extracts shows the sensible man's attitude to Authority and Tradition.

From the *Discoveries*

(*a*)

[Of the magnitude, and compass of any Fable, Epic or Dramatic.]

The Fable is called the *Imitation* [1] of one entire and perfect action; whose parts are so joined, and knit together, as nothing in the structure can be changed, or taken away, without impairing, or troubling the whole; of which there is a proportionable magnitude in the members. As for example: if a man would build a house, he would first appoint a place to build it in, which he would define within certain bounds. So in the constitution of a poem, the Action is aimed at by the poet, which answers Place in a building, and that Action hath his largeness, compass, and proportion. But, as a Court or King's Palace requires other dimensions than a private house, so the Epic asks a magnitude, from other poems. . . . By perfect, we understand that to which nothing is wanting; as Place to the building that is raised, and Action to the fable that is formed. It is perfect, perhaps, not for a Court, or King's Palace, which requires a greater ground; but for the structure we would raise, so the space of the Action may not prove large enough for the Epic Fable, yet be perfect for the Dramatic, and whole.

Whole we call that, and perfect, which hath a *beginning,* a *midst,* and an *end.* . . . Therefore, as in every body, so in every Action, which is the subject of a just work, there is required a certain proportionable greatness, neither too vast, nor too minute. For that which happens to the eyes, when we behold a body, the same happens to the memory, when we contemplate an action. I look upon a monstrous giant, as Tityus, whose body covered nine acres of land, and mine eye sticks upon every part; the whole that consists of those parts will never be taken in at one entire view. So in a Fable, if the Action be too great, we can never comprehend the whole together in our imagination. Again, if it be too little, there ariseth no pleasure out of the object; it affords the view no stay. ... Now, in every Action it behooves the poet to know which is his utmost bound, how far with fitness and a necessary proportion he may produce and determine it. That is, till either good fortune change into the worse, or the worse into the better. For as a body without proportion cannot be goodly, no more can the Action, either in Comedy or Tragedy, without his fit bounds. And every bound for the nature of the subject is esteemed the best that is largest till it can increase no more: so it behooves the Action in Tragedy or Comedy, to be let grow till the necessity ask a conclusion: wherein two things are to be considered; first, that it exceed not the compass of one day, next, that there be place left for digression and art. For the Episodes and digressions in a Fable are the same that household stuff and other furniture are in a house.

Now, that it should be one and entire. One—either as it is only separate and by itself, or as being composed of many parts, it begins to be one, as those parts grow, or are wrought together. That it should be One the first way alone, and by itself, no man that hath tasted letters ever would say. ...

So many there be of old that hath thought the Action of one man to be one; . . . which is both foolish and false; since by one and the same person many things may be severally done, which cannot fitly be referred, or joined to the same end. Virgil, writing of Aeneas . . . neither tells us how he was born, how brought up, how he fought with Achilles, how he was snatched out of the battle by Venus; but that one thing, *how he came into Italy,* he prosecutes in twelve books. The rest of his journey, his error by sea, the sack of Troy, are put not as the Argument of the work but Episodes of the Argument. So Homer laid by many things of Ulysses and handled no more than he saw tended to one and the same end.

Contrary to which and foolishly those poets did, whom the Philosopher taxeth; of whom one gathered all the actions of Theseus, another put all the labours of Hercules in one work: . . . amongst which there were many parts had no coherence, nor kindred one with other, so far they were from being one Action, one Fable. For as a house consisting of diverse materials becomes one structure and one dwelling, so an Action, composed of diverse parts, may become one Fable Epic or Dramatic. For example in a Tragedy look upon Sophocles' *Ajax*: Ajax deprived of Achilles' armour, which he hoped from the suffrage of the Greeks, disdains; and, growing impatient of the injury, rageth, and turns mad. In that humour he doth many senseless things; and at last fall's upon the Grecian flock, and kills a great ram for Ulysses. Returning to his sense, he grows ashamed of the scorn, and kills himself; and is by the chiefs of the Greeks forbidden burial. These things agree, and hang together, not as they were done; but as seeming to be done, which made the Action whole, entire and absolute.

For the whole, as it consisteth of parts; so without all the parts it is not the whole; and to make it absolute, is required, not only the parts, but such parts as are true. For a part of the whole was true; which if you take away, you either change the whole or it is not the whole. For if it be such a part, as being present or absent, nothing concerns the whole, it cannot be called a part of the whole.

(*b*)

I cannot think Nature is so spent, and decayed, that she can bring forth nothing worth her former years. She is always the same, like herself: and when she collects her strength, is abler still. Men are decayed, and studies. She is not.

I know nothing can conduce more to letters, than to examine the writings of the Ancients, and not to rest in their sole authority, or take all upon trust from them; provided the plagues of judging and pronouncing against them, be away; such as are envy, bitterness, precipitation, impudence, and scurrile scoffing. For to all the observations of the Ancients we have our own experience: which, if we will use, and apply, we have better means to pronounce. It is true they opened the gates, and made the way that went before us; but as Guides, not Commanders. Truth lies open to all; it is no man's several.[2]. . .

I take this labour in teaching others, that they should not be always to be taught; and I would bring my precepts into practice. For rules are ever of less force and value than experiments. Yet with this purpose, rather to show the right way to those that come after than to detect any that have slipped before by error, and I hope it will be more profitable. For men do more willingly listen and with more favour to precept than reprehension. Among diverse opinions of an art, and most of them contrary in themselves, it is hard to make election; and therefore though a man cannot invent new things after so many, he may do a welcome work yet to help posterity to judge rightly of the old. But arts and precepts avail nothing, except Nature be beneficial and aiding. And therefore these things are no more written to a dull disposition than rules of husbandry to a barren soil. No precepts will profit a fool, no more than beauty will the blind, or music the deaf. ...

Nothing is more ridiculous than to make an author a dictator, as the schools have done Aristotle. The damage is infinite, knowledge receives by it. For to many things a man should owe but a temporary belief, and a suspension of his own judgment, not an absolute resignation of himself, or a perpetual captivity. Let Aristotle, and others, have their dues: but if we can make farther discoveries of truth and fitness than they, why are we envied? Let us beware, while we strive to add, we do not diminish, or deface; we may improve, but not augment. By discrediting falsehood, Truth grows in request. We must not go about like men anguished and perplexed for vicious affectation of praise: but calmly study the separation of opinions, find the errors have intervened, awake Antiquity, call former times into question, but make no parties[3] with the present, nor follow any fierce undertakers,[4] mingle no matter of doubtful credit with the simplicity of truth, but gently stir the mould about the root of the question, and avoid all digladiations,[5] facility of credit, or superstitious simplicity; seek the consonance and concatenation of Truth; stoop only to point of necessity, and what leads to convenience. Then make exact animadversion where style hath flourished, and thrived in choiceness of phrase, round and clean composition of sentence, sweet falling of the clause, varying an illustration by tropes [6] and figures, weight of matter, worth of subject, soundness of argument, life of invention, and depth of judgment. This is *Monte potiri,* to get the hill. For no perfect Discovery can be made upon a flat or a level. . . .

I am not of that opinion to conclude a poet's liberty within the narrow limits of laws, which either the grammarians or the philosophers prescribe. For, before they found out those laws, there were many excellent poets that fulfilled them. Amongst whom none more perfect than Sophocles, who lived a little before Aristotle.

Which of the Greeklings durst ever give precepts to Demosthenes? or to Pericles (whom the age surnamed *heavenly,* because he seemed to thunder, and lighten, with his language)? or to Alcibiades, who had rather Nature for his guide, than Art for his master?

But whatsoever Nature at any time dictated to the most happy, or long exercise to the most laborious, that the wisdom and learning of Aristotle hath brought into an art; because he understood the causes of things: and what other men did by chance or custom, he doth by reason; and not only found out the way not to err, but the short way we should take, not to err.

Many things in Euripides hath Aristophanes wittily reprehended; not out of Art, but out of Truth. For, Euripides is sometimes peccant, as he is most times perfect. But, Judgment when it is greatest, if Reason doth not accompany it, is not ever absolute.

To judge of poets is only the faculty of poets; and not of all poets, but the best. But, some will say, critics are a kind of tinkers, that make more faults than they mend ordinarily. See their diseases, and those of grammarians. It is true, many bodies are the worse for the meddling with: and the multitude of physicians hath destroyed many sound patients with their wrong practice. But the office of a true critic, or censor, is not to throw by a letter anywhere, or damn an innocent syllable, but lay the words together, and amend them; judge sincerely of the author, and his matter, which is the sign of solid and perfect learning in a man. Such was Horace, an author of much civility, and (if any one among the heathen can be) the best master both of virtue and wisdom; an excellent and true judge upon cause and reason, not because he thought so, but because he knew so, out of use and experience.

(*c*)

I remember the Players have often mentioned it as an honour to Shakespeare that in his writing (whatsoever he penned) he never blotted out line. My answer hath been, would he had blotted a thousand. Which they thought a malevolent speech. I had not told posterity this, but for their ignorance, who chose that circumstance to commend their friend by, wherein he most faulted. And to justify mine own candour, (for I loved the man, and do honour his memory on this side Idolatry as much as any). He was (indeed) honest, and of an open, and free nature: had an excellent phantasy, brave notions, and gentle expressions: wherein he flowed with that facility that sometimes it was necessary he should be stopped: *sufflaminandus erat,* as Augustus said of Haterius. His wit was in his own power; would the rule of it had been so too! Many times he fell into those things could not escape laughter: as when he said in the person of Cæsar, one speaking to him *Cæsar thou dost me wrong,* he replied: *Cæsar never did wrong, but with just cause*: and such like, which were ridiculous. But he redeemed his vices with his virtues. There was ever more in him to be praised than to be pardoned.

(*a*)

[1]*Imitation.*—"If we wonder why Aristotle, and Plato before him, should lay such stress on the theory that art is imitation,

it is a help to realise that common language called it 'making' and it was clearly not 'making' in the ordinary sense. The poet who was 'maker 'of a Fall of Troy clearly did not make the real Fall of Troy. He made an imitation Fall of Troy."—*G. Murray.* So "imitate" almost means "depict." It must be remembered that Greek tragedy and epic (but not Comedy, which Aristotle forgets or overlooks) did not attempt to invent stories or themes, but simply gave the old myths and stories a new life in art.

(*b*)

[2]*several*—private property, *i.e.,* it is common land.
[3]*make no parties*—*i.e.,* take no sides, join no factions.
[4]*undertakers*— "fans."
[5]*digladiations* — "sword fights"—*i.e.,* debates, contentions.
[6]*tropes* — "turns of speech" — and so "figures of speech."

4

Dryden

John Dryden (1631-1700) was the outstanding writer of the end of the seventeenth century. At the time of his death it could be said that he had established the heroic couplet as the proper instrument for the age that he had written satires worthy to be judged alongside those of Rome, and that his plays, including *All for Love* (1678), made his age proud of its drama. The admirer of Dryden would further remind you of his Odes, his allegory *The Hind and the Panther,* his translation of Virgil, and his critical essays. Whatever branch of literature he attempted, he seemed to carry to greater heights of strength and beauty.

One of his greatest achievements was his creation of a new and improved language for verse. "He found the language brick and left it marble." He saw that English poetry, if it were to develop, must recover some of the properties of prose—clarity, directness, vigour. He restored to prose—"the other harmony"—some of the musical properties of verse. His prose delights the ear as well as the mind.

His *Essay of Dramatic Poetry* (1668) is the source of most of the extracts that follow. He takes pride in the literature that England has created, answering her own needs, and refuses to allow that it is inferior to that of France. He talks of literature naturally and with the interest of one, who loves his subject and knows its importance. His power of searching analysis and his delight in clear statement are strengthened by his gracious manner, his sincerity, his reasonableness. He talks to us intimately, with the ease of a gentleman and the kindliness of a friend. He is sufficiently serene and clear-sighted to allow merits in writers of other schools and other countries, and to acknowledge flaws in those he admires.

The framework of this Essay (written "to vindicate the honour of our English writers from the censure of those who unjustly prefer the French") is this: four friends— Crites, Eugenius, Neander, Lisideius—chat as they sail up the river Thames. Neander represents himself—the others give the views of serious-minded contemporaries. Crites (Sir Robert Howard) is a noted opponent of rhyme in plays. Dryden follows the style of the Socratic dialogue—"sustained by persons of several opinions, all of them left doubtful, to be determined by the readers in general." He would not be thought "naturally guilty of so much vanity as to dictate" his opinions. This Essay is an important contribution to criticism, the considered opinions of a man of true judgment. The prose is that of an artist.

(*a*)

Preface to *Almanzor and Almahide*, 1670

Whether heroic verse ought to be admitted into serious plays is not now to be disputed; it is already in possession of the stage, and I dare confidently affirm that very few tragedies, in this age, shall be received without it. All the arguments which are formed against it can amount to no more than this: that it is not so near conversation as prose, and therefore not so natural. But it is very clear to all who understand poetry, that serious plays ought not to imitate conversation too early. If nothing were to be raised above that level, the foundation of poetry would be destroyed. And if you once admit of a latitude that thoughts may be exalted, and that images and actions may be raised above the life, and described in measure without rhyme, that leads you insensibly from your own principles to mine; you are already so far onward of your way, that you have forsaken the imitation of ordinary converse. You are gone beyond it; and to continue where you are to lodge in the open fields, betwixt two inns. You have lost that which you call natural, and have not acquired the last perfection of art. But it was only custom which cozened us so long; we thought, because Shakespeare and Fletcher went no further, that there the pillars of poetry were to be erected; that, because they excellently described passion without rhyme, therefore rhyme was not capable of describing it. But time has now convinced most men of that error. It is indeed so difficult to write verse, that the adversaries of it have a good plea against many who undertook that task, without being formed by art or nature for it. Yet, even they, who have written worst in it, would have written worse without it: they have cozened many with their sound, who never took the pains to examine their sense. In fine, they have succeeded; though, it is true, they have more dishonoured rhyme by their good success than they have done by their ill. But I am willing to let fall this argument. It is free for every man to write, or not to write, in verse, as he judges it to be, or not to be, his talent; or as he imagines the audience will receive it.

(*b*) From the *Essay of Dramatic Poetry*

Neander. I acknowledge that the French contrive their plots more regularly, and observe the laws of comedy, and decorum of the stage (to speak generally) with more exactness than the English. Farther, I deny not but he has taxed us justly in some irregularities of ours, which he has mentioned; yet, after all, I am of opinion that neither our faults nor their virtues are considerable enough to place them above us.

For the lively imitation of nature being in the definition of a play,[1] these which best fulfill that law ought to be esteemed superior to the others. 'Tis true, those beauties of the French poesy are such as will raise perfection higher where it is, but are not sufficient to give it where it is not: they are indeed the beauties of a statue, but not of a man, because not animated with the soul of poesy, which is imitation of humour and passions.

. . . But of late years Moliére, the younger Corneille, Quinault, and some others, have been imitating afar off the quick turns and graces of the English stage. They have mixed their serious plays with mirth, like our tragi-comedies. ... But their humours[2] . . . are so thin-sown, that never above one of them comes up in any play. I dare take upon me to find more variety of them in some one play of Ben Jonson's than in all theirs together. . . . As for their new way of mingling mirth with serious plot, I do not, with Lisideius, condemn the thing, though I cannot approve their manner of doing it. He tells us we cannot so speedily recollect ourselves after a scene of great passion and concernment, as to pass to another of mirth and humour, and to enjoy it with any relish; but why should he imagine the soul of man more heavy than his senses? Does not the eye pass from an unpleasant object to a pleasant in a much shorter time than is required to this? And does not the unpleasantness of the first commend the beauty of the latter? The old rule of logic might have convinced him that contraries, when placed near, set off each other. A continued gravity keeps the spirit too much bent; we must refresh it sometimes, as we bait in a journey, that we may go on with greater ease. A scene of mirth, mixed with tragedy, has the same effect upon us which our music has betwixt the acts; which we find a relief to us from the best plots and language of the stage, if the discourses have been long. I must therefore have stronger arguments, here I am convinced that compassion and mirth in the same subject destroy each other; and in the meantime cannot but conclude, to the honour of our nation, that we have invented,[3] increased, and perfected a more pleasant way of writing for the stage, than was known to the ancients or moderns of any nation, which is tragi-comedy.

And this leads me to wonder why Lisideius and many others should cry up the barrenness of the French plots above the variety and copiousness of the English. Their plots are single; they carry on one design, which is pushed forward by all the actors, every scene in the play contributing and moving towards it. Our plays, besides the main design, have under-plots or by-concernments, of less considerable persons and intrigues, which are carried on with the motion of the main plot: as they say the orb of the fixed stars, and those of the planets, though they have motions of their own, are whirled about by the motion of the *primum mobile* in which they are contained.

As for his other argument, that by pursuing one single theme they gain an advantage to express and work up the passions, I wish any example he could bring from them would make it good;

for I confess their verses are to me the coldest I have ever read. Neither, indeed, is it possible for them, in the way they take, so to express passion, as that the effects of it should appear in the concernment of an audience, their speeches being so many declamations, which tire us with the length. . . . But to speak generally; it cannot be denied that short speeches and replies are more apt to move the passions and beget concernment in us than the other; for it is unnatural for any one in a gust of passion to speak long together, or for another in the same condition to suffer him, without interruption. Grief and passion are like floods raised in little brooks by a sudden rain; they are quickly up; and if the concernment be poured unexpectedly in upon us, it overflows us: but a long sober shower gives them leisure to run out as they came in, without troubling the ordinary current. As for comedy, repartee is one of its chiefest graces; the greatest pleasure of the audience is a chace of wit,[4] kept up on both sides and swiftly managed. And this our forefathers, if not we, have had in Fletcher's plays, to a much higher degree of perfection than the French poets can reasonably hope to reach.

There is another part of Lisideius his discourse, in which he has rather excused our neighbours than commended them; that is, for aiming only to make one person considerable in their plays. 'Tis very true what he has urged, that one character in all plays, even without the poet's care, will have advantage of all the others; and that the design of the whole drama will chiefly depend on it. But this hinders not that there may be more shining characters in the play: many persons of a second magnitude, nay, some so very near, so almost equal to the first, that greatness may be opposed to greatness, and all the persons be made considerable, not only by their quality but by their action. 'Tis evident that the more the persons are, the greater will be the variety of the plot. If then the parts are managed so regularly that the beauty of the whole be kept entire, and that the variety become not a perplexed and confused mass of accidents, you will find it infinitely pleasing to be led in a labyrinth of design, where you see some of your way before you, yet discern not the end till you arrive at it. And that all this is practicable, I can produce for examples many of our English plays: as *The Maid's Tragedy*,[5] *The Alchemist*, *The Silent Woman*.[6]. . .

I must acknowledge that the French have reason to hide that part of the action which would occasion too much tumult on the stage, and to choose rather to have it made known by narration to the audience. Farther, I think it very convenient that all incredible actions were removed; but, whether custom has so insinuated itself into our countrymen,[7] or nature has so formed them to fierceness, I know not; but they will scarcely suffer combats and other acts of horror to be taken from them. And indeed, the indecency of tumults is all which can be objected against fighting: for why may not our imagination as well suffer itself to be deluded[8] with the probability of it, as with any other thing in the play? For my part, I can with as great ease persuade myself that the blows are given in good earnest, as I can that they who strike them are kings and princes, or those persons which they represent. ... To conclude on this subject of relations; if we are to be blamed for shewing too much of the action, the French are as faulty for discovering too little of it: a mean betwixt both should be observed by every judicious writer, so as the audience may neither be left unsatisfied by not seeing what is beautiful, or shocked by beholding what is either incredible or undecent.

. . . We have borrowed nothing from them; our plots are weaved in English looms: we endeavour therein to follow the greatness of characters which are derived to us from Shakespeare and Fletcher; the copiousness and well-knitting of the intrigues we have from Jonson; and for the verse itself we have English precedents of elder date[9] than any of Corneille's plays.

... I dare boldly affirm[10] these two things of the English drama: First, that we have many plays of ours as regular as any of theirs, and which, besides, have more variety of plot and characters; and, secondly, that in most of the irregular plays of Shakespeare or Fletcher, (for Ben Jonson's are for the most part regular) there is a more masculine fancy and greater spirit in the writing than there is in any of the French.

[Shakespeare.][11] He was the man who of all modern, and perhaps ancient poets, had the largest and most comprehensive soul. All the images of nature were still present to him, and he drew them, not laboriously, but luckily; when he describes anything, you more than see it, you feel it too. Those who accuse him to have wanted learning, give him the greater commendation: he was naturally learned; he needed not the spectacles of books to read nature; he looked inwards and found her there. I cannot say he is everywhere alike; were he so, I should do him injury to compare him with the greatest of mankind. He is many times flat, insipid; his comic wit degenerating into clenches, his serious swelling into bombast. But he is always great, when some great occasion is presented to him; no man can say he ever had a fit subject for his wit, and did not then raise himself as high above the rest of poets "as the cypress towers above the bending shrubs."

(*a*)

On this question of rhyme in plays, Dryden wrote: "None are very violent against it, but those who either have not attempted it, or who have succeeded ill in their attempt." He insisted that in using rhyme he was no servile imitator of the French, but continued the native tradition, temporarily broken by Shakespeare, resumed by Davenant's *Siege of Rhodes* (1656) in heroic couplets. Howard himself wrote plays in rhyme, to be followed by Dryden. The plays themselves were different from those of the later Elizabethans, and their distinctive qualities have given them the name "Heroic Drama"—with "their involved plots, extravagant incidents, swelling metaphors and similes." Of them a Frenchman writes: "There are no characters, only extremely effective situations allowing of high-sounding, pompous speeches." To those to whom rhetoric and declamation appealed, the heroic drama was the ideal outlet, and the rhymed couplet the ideal vehicle of expression.

In the *Essay of Dramatic Poetry,* Dryden makes Crites state the case against rhyme in plays.

1. No plays in rhyme can be found to challenge "those excellent plays of Shakespeare, Fletcher, and Ben Jonson which have been written out of rhyme."
2. "Rhyme is unnatural in a play, because dialogue there is presented as the effect of sudden thought: for a play is the imitation of nature; and since no man, without premeditation, speaks in rhyme, neither ought he to do it on the stage." Tragedy should be written in the form of

verse nearest prose that still allows elevation of thought and language--*i.e.,* blank verse. "The hand of art will be too visible in" rhyme.

3. "Rhyme is uncapable of expressing the greatest thoughts naturally, and the lowest it cannot with any grace." (Fancy telling a servant in rhyme to shut the door!)
4. "A quick and luxuriant fancy which would extend itself too far on every subject" is sufficiently circumscribed by verse without rhyme.

In the same essay Neander [Dryden] would limit the use of rhyme to tragedy—"serious plays where the subject and characters are great." He does not advocate writing the whole of a play in closed couplets. "The necessity of a rhyme never forces any but bad or lazy writers to say what they would not otherwise. . . . Rhyme might be made as natural as blank verse, by the well-placing of the words." As for the challenge to produce rhymed plays equal to Shakespeare and Fletcher," not only we shall never equal them, but they could not equal themselves, were they to rise and write again." So that the writers of his age must cease from writing or find a new way. "This way of writing in verse they have only left free to us." "Tragedy is wont to image to us the minds and fortunes of noble persons, and to portray these exactly; heroic rhyme is nearest nature, as being the noblest kind of modern verse." If rhyme is improper for tragedy, then it must be improper for epic too. " A play, to be like nature, is set above it; as statues which are placed on high are made greater than the life, that they may descend to the sight in their just proportion." He admits that the hand of art is apparent in repartee in rhyme, but claims that other beauties rob us of sense of labour in the rhyme itself. As for saying "Shut the door" in rhyme, the need seldom arose and excused the fault, if it were a fault to express the idea in lofty language. Many of the best writers needed the bonds of rhyme as well as of verse. "Judgment is indeed the master-workman in a play; but he requires many subordinate hands, many tools to his assistance. And verse I affirm to be one of these; 'tis a rule and line by which he keeps his building compact and even, which otherwise lawless imagination would raise either irregularly or loosely."

(*b*)

[1]*definition of a play*—that of Lisideius at the opening—"A just and lively image of human nature, representing its passions and humours, and the changes of fortune to which it is subject, for the delight and instruction of mankind." For Imitation=Representation, see note to Ben Jonson, p. 21. The mention of 'delight' *before* 'instruction' is a noteworthy advance.

[2]*humours*—here used as vivid representations of character, as in the later plays of Ben Jonson rather than the earlier manner of *Every Man in his Humour* in which each character seemed to have one whim or oddness exaggerated to the exclusion of all others.

[3]*we have invented* [tragi-comedy].—It is claimed that the earliest Spanish example was written before 1490.

[4]*chace of wit*—like a long rally in tennis.

[5]*The Maid's Tragedy,* by Beaumont and Fletcher.

[6]*The Alchemist, The Silent Woman*, by Ben Jonson.

[7]*our countrymen.*—Dryden was one of the first to discuss English writings as something peculiarly fitted to and expressive of the English spirit.

[8]*our imagination . . . deluded.*—Another passage in which Dryden anticipated Coleridge's theory (see 4 (c) Questions, p. 161) is in his *Defence of the Essay of Dramatic Poetry:* "Imagination in a man or reasonable creature is supposed to participate of reason; and when that governs, as it does in the belief of fiction, reason is not destroyed, but misled, or blinded: . . . reason suffers itself to be so hoodwinked, that it may better enjoy the pleasures of the fiction."

[9]*English precedents of elder date.*—"Ralph Roister Doister," "Gammer Gurton's Needle" are in twelve syllabled lines; "The Misogonus" (c. 1560) in lines of fourteen syllables, rhyming alternately.

[10]*I dare boldly affirm.*—One of the starting-points of the conversation was the claim of Eugenius: "There is no man more ready to adore these great Greeks and Romans than I am: but on the other side, I cannot think so contemptibly of the age in which I live, or so dishonourably of my own country, as not to judge we equal the ancients in most kinds of poesy, and in some

surpass them; neither know I any reason why I may not be as zealous for the reputation of our age, as we find the ancients themselves were in reference to those who lived before them."

[11]*Shakespeare.*—In a Preface to *Troilus and Cressida,* spoken by Mr. Betterton, representing the Ghost of Shakespeare, Dryden makes Shakespeare say:

"Untaught, unpractised, in a barbarous age,
I found not, but created first the stage.
And, if I drained no Greek or Latin store,
'T was, that my own abundance gave me more.
On foreign trade I needed not rely,
Like fruitful Britain, rich without supply."

5

Pope

Alexander Pope (1688-1744) chose to be a poet, and began early to practise the art. His inborn ear for fine effects in verse was his greatest asset. A friend advised him: "We have had great poets, but never one great poet that was correct." It was a time when chaos and upheaval were dreaded: the people wanted order and stability. Dryden's lucidity and rationality pointed the way, and Pope elected to perfect the poetry of sense and taste and order. He devoted himself to his art, serving literature not for power or place or pay, but partly for fame and largely for her own sake. In his *Essay on Criticism,* (1711), *The Rape of the Lock* (1714), his translations of the Iliad and the Odyssey, *The Dunciad* (1728), and the: *Essay on Man* (1733), he established himself as the supreme poet of his day, and the heroic couplet as the right vehicle for the matter of his times.

The *Essay on Criticism* is first of all a poem, a brilliant piece of craftsmanship delighting the intellect, full of felicities of expression. Further, it is the first attempt in English literature at "anything like a complete exposition of stylistic criticism." It is an important expression of the beliefs of the writer and the spirit of the age. Writers of the day felt with Pope that "all that is left us is to recommend our productions by the imitation of the ancients." Years had to elapse before anyone dared to retaliate "The less we copy the renowned ancients, we shall resemble them the more" (Young). The superiority of the classics overwhelmed writers, who felt that there were no new worlds to conquer, only old ones to civilise and improve. Thus, what was needed was expounders of the prophets of old, not visionaries with disturbing inspirations. The wisest dicta on the art of writing were to be found in Aristotle, Longinus, Horace, Boileau. Pope collected them, arranged them, and displayed them in pointed verse which made the inspiration of the past lucid and memorable. This 'anthology,' in which originality was confined to expression, supplied a demand and strengthened the taste for knowing and following the rules of the game.

Addison acclaimed it in *The Spectator* as "a masterpiece of its kind. ... It is impossible for us, who live in the latter ages of the world, to make observations in criticism, morality, or in any art or science, which have not been touched upon by others. We have little else left us but to represent the common sense of mankind in more stronger, more beautiful, or more uncommon lights." As that was the feeling of the time, Pope's Essay was bound to succeed and to establish more firmly the power of authority and tradition. Pope struck a blow for Reason and Classicism, the effects of which survived for a long time. Now we agree that we need both the authority of tradition and "the liberty of genius to seek new conquests." Even now we cannot agree about the proportions of the two apparently discordant elements. The Age of Pope had no such doubts: it staked all on the old gods and readily accepted the triple yoke of 'Nature, Reason, and the Ancients.'

In the work of this man of twenty-three, revolutionary doctrines or startlingly new interpretations are not to be expected. He limits himself to Poetry—the region he knew. He writes not to instruct a genius but to enable men of taste and good sense—*i.e.*, those whom Poetry should aim at pleasing—the true arbiters, to recognise and applaud Talent, to value order, sense, strength, exactness, and freshness of expression higher than mere display of technical dexterity and empty tunefulness.

'Nature' to Pope is almost identical with Reason. Nature, he seems to argue, is perfect. The Ancients possessed Nature's secret, and Nature is seen to perfection in their works because their art always accorded with Reason. Their laws—always present—were not imposed: the Ancients, creatures of Reason, found them. The Ancients should be followed, not because they were divinely inspired, but because they worked by the light of Reason. Thus Poetry can be tested by Antiquity, Nature, and Reason—a formidable trinity.

From the *Essay on Criticism*

(*a*)

'Tis with our judgments as our watches, none
Go just alike, yet each believes his own.
In poets, as true genius is but rare,
True taste as seldom is the critic's share;
Both must alike from heav'n derive their light,
These born to judge, as well as those to write.
Let such teach others who themselves excel,
And censure freely who have written well.
. . . But you who seek to give and merit fame,
And justly bear a critic's noble name,
Be sure yourself and your own reach to know,
How far your genius, taste, and learning go;
Launch not beyond your depth, but be discreet,
And mark that point where sense and dullness meet.

(*b*)

First follow **Nature**, and your judgment frame
By her just standard, which is still the same:
Unerring Nature, still divinely bright,
One clear, unchang'd, and universal light,
Life, force and beauty, must to all impart,
At once the source, and end, and test of art.
Art from that fund each just supply provides,
Works without show, and without pomp presides:
In some fair body thus th' informing soul
With spirits feeds, with vigour fills the whole,
Each motion guides, and ev'ry nerve sustains;
Itself unseen, but in th' effects, remains.
Some, to whom heav'n in wit has been profuse,

Want as much more, to turn it to its use;
For wit and judgment often are at strife,
Tho' meant each other's aid, like man and wife.
'Tis more to guide, than spur the Muse's steed;
Restrain his fury, than provoke his speed;
The winged courser, like a gen'rous horse,
Shows most true mettle when you check his course.
  Those **Rules** of old, discover'd, not devis'd,
Are Nature still, but Nature methodiz'd;
Nature, like liberty, is but restrain'd
By the same laws which first herself ordain'd.
  Hear how learn'd Greece her useful rules incites,
When to repress, and when indulge our flights:
High on Parnassus' top her sons she show'd,
And pointed out those arduous paths they trod;
Held from afar, aloft, th' immortal prize,
And urged the rest by equal steps to rise.
Just precepts thus from great examples giv'n,
She drew from them what they deriv'd from heav'n.
The gen'rous critic fann'd the poet's fire,
And taught the world with reason to admire.
Then criticism the Muse's handmaid prov'd,
To dress her charms, and make her more belov'd:
But following wits from that intention stray'd;
Who could not win the mistress, woo'd the maid;
Against the poets their own arms they turn'd,
Sure to hate most the men from whom they learn'd.
So modern 'pothecaries, taught the art
By doctor's bills to play the doctor's part,
Bold in the practice of mistaken rules,
Prescribe, apply, and call their masters fools.
Some on the leaves of ancient authors prey;
Nor time nor moths e'er spoil'd so much as they:
Some drily plain, without invention's aid,
Write dull receipts how poems may be made.
These leave the sense, their learning to display,

And those explain the meaning quite away.
  You then whose judgment the right course would steer,
Know well each **Ancient's** proper character;
His fable, subject, scope in ev'ry page;
Religion, country, genius of his age:
Witnout all these at once before your eyes,
Cavil you may, but never criticize.
Be Homer's works your study and delight,
Read them by day, and meditate by night;
Thence form your judgment, thence your maxims bring,
And trace the Muses upward to their spring;
Still with itself compar'd, his text peruse;
And let your comment be the Mantuan Muse.[1]
  When first young Maro[1] in his boundless mind
A work t' outlast immortal Rome design'd,
Perhaps he seem'd above the critic's law,
And but from Nature's fountains scorned to draw:
But when t' examine ev'ry part he came,
Nature and Homer were, he found, the same.
Convinc'd, amaz'd, he checks the bold design;
And rules as strict his labour'd work confine,
As if the Stagirite [2] o'erlook'd each line.
Learn hence for ancient rules a just esteem;
To copy Nature is to copy them.
  Some beauties yet no precepts can declare,
For there's a happiness as well as care.
Music resembles poetry; in each
Are nameless graces which no methods teach,
And which a master-hand alone can reach.
If, where the rules not far enough extend
(Since rules were made but to promote their end),
Some lucky Licence answer to the full
Th' intent propos'd, that licence is a rule.
Thus Pegasus, a nearer way to take,
May boldly deviate from the common track.
Great wits sometimes may gloriously offend

And rise to faults true critics dare not mend;
From vulgar bounds with brave disorder part,
And snatch a grace beyond the reach of art,
Which, without passing thro' the judgment, gains
The heart, and all its end at once attains.
In prospects thus, some objects please our eyes,
Which out of Nature's common order rise,
The shapeless rock, or hanging precipice.
But tho' the ancients thus their rules invade
(As kings dispense with laws themselves have made),
Moderns, beware! Or if you must offend
Against the precept, ne'er transgress its end;
Let it be seldom, and compell'd by need;
And have, at least, their precedent to plead.
The critic else proceeds without remorse
Seizes your frame, and puts his laws in force.

(*c*)

A perfect judge will read each work of wit
With the same spirit that its author writ:
Survey the whole, nor seek slight faults to find
Where Nature moves, and rapture warms the mind;
Nor lose, for that malignant dull delight,
The gen'rous pleasure to be charmed with wit.
But in such plays as neither ebb, nor flow,
Correctly cold, and regularly low,
That shunning faults one quiet tenor keep;
We cannot blame indeed—but we may sleep.
In wit, as nature, what affects our hearts?
Is not th' exactness of peculiar parts;
'Tis not a lip, or eye, we beauty call,
But the joint force and full result of all.
Thus when we view some well-proportion'd dome
(The world's just wonder, and ev'n thine, O Rome!),
No single parts unequally surprise,

All comes united to th' admiring eyes;
No monstrous height, or breadth, or length appears;
The whole at once is bold, and regular.
  Whoever thinks a faultless piece to see,
Thinks what ne'er was, nor is, nor e'er shall be.
In ev'ry work regards the writer's end,
Since none can compass more than they intend;
And if the means be just, the conduct true,
Applause, in spite of trivial faults, is due;
As men of breeding, sometimes men of wit,
T' avoid great errors, must the less commit:
Neglect the rules each verbal critic lays,
For not to know some trifles, is a praise.
Most critics, fond of some subservient art,
Still make the whole depend upon a part:
They talk of principles, but notions prize,
And all to one lov'd folly sacrifice.
Thus critics, of less judgment than caprice,
Curious, riot knowing, not exact but nice,
Form short ideas; and offend in arts
(As most in manners) by a love to parts.
  Some to *Conceit*[3] alone their taste confine,
And glitt'ring thoughts struck out at ev'ry line;
Pleas'd with a work where nothing's just or fit,
One glaring chaos and wild heap of wit.
Poets, like painters, thus unskill'd to trace
The naked nature and the living grace,
With gold and jewels cover ev'ry part,
And hide with ornaments their want of art.
True *wit*[4] is Nature to advantage dressed,
What oft was thought, but ne'er so well expressed;
Something, whose truth convinc'd at sight we find,
That gives us back the image of our mind.
As shades more sweetly recommend the light,
So modest plainness sets off sprightly wit.
For works may have more wit than does 'em good,

As bodies perish through excess of blood.
  Others for *language* all their care express,
And value books, as women, men, for dress:
Their praise is still—the style is excellent;
The sense, they humbly take upon content.
Words are like leaves; and where they most abound,
Much fruit of sense beneath is rarely found.
False eloquence, like the prismatic glass,
Its gaudy colours spreads on ev'ry place;
The face of Nature we no more survey,
All glares alike, without distinction gay:
But true expression, like th' unchanging sun,
Clears and improves whate'er it shines upon,
It gilds all objects but it alters none.
Expression is the dress of thought, and still
Appears more decent, as more suitable;
A vile conceit in pompous words expressed
Is like a clown in regal purple dressed:
For diff'rent styles with diffe'rent subjects sort,
As several garbs with country, town, and court.
Some by old words to fame have made pretence,
Ancients in phrase, mere moderns in their sense;
Such labour'd nothings, in so strange a style,
Amaze th' unlearned, and make the learned smile.
Unlucky, as Fungoso[5] in the play,
These sparks with awkward vanity display
What the fine gentleman wore yesterday!
And but so mimic ancient wits at best,
As apes our grandsires, in their doublets dressed.
In words, as fashions, the same rule will hold,
Alike fantastic, if too new, or old:
Be not the first by whom the new are tried,
Nor yet the last to lay the old aside.
  But most by *numbers*[6] judge a poet's song,
And smooth or rough, with them, is right or wrong

In the bright Muse tho' thousand charms conspire,
Her voice is all these tuneful fools admire;
Who haunt Parnassus but to please their ear?
Not mend their minds; as some to church repair,
Not for the doctrine, but the music there.
These equal syllables alone require,
Tho' oft the ear the open vowels tire;
While expletives their feeble aid do join,
And ten low words oft creep in one dull line:
While they ring round the same unvaried chimes,
With sure returns of still expected rhymes;
Where'er you find "the cooling western breeze,"
In the next line, it "whispers thro' the trees":
If "crystal streams with pleasing murmurs creep,"
The reader's threaten'd (not in vain) with "sleep":
Then, at the last and only couplet fraught
With some unmeaning thing they call a thought,
A needless Alexandrine[7] ends the song,
That, like a wounded snake, drags its slow length along.
Leave such to tune their own dull rhymes, and know
What's roundly smooth or languishingly slow;
And praise the easy vigour of a line,
Where Denham's strength, and Waller's sweetness join.
True ease in writing comes from art, not chance,
As those move easiest who have learn'd to dance.
'Tis not enough no harshness gives offence,
The sound must seem an echo to the sense:
Soft is the strain when Zephyr gently blows,
And the smooth stream in smoother numbers flows;
But when loud surges lash the sounding shore,
The hoarse, rough verse should like the torrent roar:
When Ajax strives some rock's vast weight to throw,
The line too labours, and the words move slow;
Not so, when swift Camilla scours the plain,
Flies o'er th' unbending corn, and skims along the main.

[1]*the Mantuan muse . . . young Maro.*—Virgil.

[2]*the Stagirite.*—Aristotle.

[3]*Conceit*—fanciful thought, startling analogy.

[4]*wit*—stimulating but satisfying expression of a thought.

[5]*Fungoso*—in *Every Man out of his Humour,* he failed to pass himself off as an utterly different character.

[6]*numbers*—verses.

[7]*Alexandrine*—an iambic line of twelve syllables.

6

Eighteenth-century Essayists

After the repeal of the Licensing Act in 1682, which ended the Government's monopoly of publishing periodicals, there arose several organs for giving the news of the day and for conducting Party warfare. On 12th April 1709 was born a new publication, intended for the general reader, the man (and woman) of taste and leisure—*The Tatler,* created by Richard Steele (1672-1729), writing under a pseudonym. He called in Joseph Addison (1672-1719), who helped to make the essay the main feature. *The Tatler* was immediately followed by *The Spectator,* which for 555 days entertained and instructed its many readers. Politics were excluded: instead, he offered "such writings as tend to the wearing out of ignorance, passion, and prejudice." "I have resolved to refresh their memories from day to day, till I have recovered them out of that desperate state of vice and folly into which the age is fallen. ... I shall be ambitious to have it said of me, that I have brought Philosophy out of closets and libraries, schools and colleges, to dwell in clubs and assemblies, at tea-tables, and in coffee-houses." In terms of circulation and influence it was a success. *The Spectator* was followed by *The Guardian.* Dr. Johnson attempted to repeat their success in *The Rambler* [1759].

In the earlier ventures Addison was always the leading figure. He contributed more than Steele, and directed the work of the other helpers. He proved by example that reforms could be made not by dogmatising or preaching, but by sugaring the pill so well that readers were laughed out of their follies. Thus by good sense and tact he became something of a censor of morals, manners, literature, and art. Much was due to his graceful style, always smooth to read and easy to understand, and the serene gentlemanliness of his attitude to his readers. The charm lay, says Mr. Gosse, "in the unaffected way with which they said perfectly simple things in the straightforward language of well-bred people."

The critical essays show Addison as something of a pioneer. He devoted many papers to a sympathetic and enlightened examination of *Paradise Lost,* at a time when Milton was diminishing in popularity. He led rather than followed the taste of his day in praising *Chevy Chase* and other old ballads. In the essays we look for, and find, sincerity rather than depth, soundness rather than brilliance. They are perfect expressions of the age marked by the individuality of the sanest representatives. They created a body of general readers with a real interest in literature and criticism, and in that body the essays helped to create good taste based on knowledge and understanding instead of on hearsay and prejudice.

(*a*) *Taste* (Addison)

Gratian very often recommends *the fine taste* as the utmost perfection of an accomplished man. As this word arises very often in conversation, I shall endeavour to give some account of it, and to lay down rules how we may know whether we are possessed of it, and how we may acquire that fine taste for writing which is so much talked of among the polite world.

Most languages make use of this metaphor to express that faculty of the mind which distinguishes all the most concealed faults and nicest perfections in writing. We may be sure this metaphor would not have been so general in all tongues, had there not been a very great conformity between that mental taste which is the subject of this paper, and that sensitive taste which gives us a relish for every different flavour that affects the palate. Accordingly, we find there are as many degrees of refinement in the intellectual faculty, as in the sense which is marked out by this common denomination.

I knew a person, who possessed the one in so great a perfection, that, after having tasted ten different kinds of tea, he would distinguish, without seeing the colour of it, the particular sort which was offered him; and not only so, but any two sorts of them that were mixed together in an equal proportion; nay, he has carried the experiment so far, as, upon tasting the composition of three different sorts, to name the parcels from whence the three several ingredients were taken. A man of a fine taste in writing will discern after the same manner, not only the general beauties and imperfections of an author, but discover the several ways of thinking and expressing himself which diversify him from all other authors, with the several foreign infusions of thought and language, and the particular authors from whom they were borrowed.

After having thus far explained what is generally meant by a fine taste in writing, and shewn the propriety of the metaphor which is used on this occasion, I think I may define it to be, *that faculty of the soul, which discerns the beauties of an author with pleasure, and the imperfections with dislike.* If a man would know whether he is possessed of this faculty, I would have him read over the celebrated works of antiquity, which have stood the test of so many different ages and countries, or those works among the moderns which have the sanction of the politer part of our contemporaries. If, upon the perusal of such writings, he does not find himself delighted in an extraordinary manner, or if, upon reading the admired passages in such authors, he finds a coldness and indifference in his thoughts, he ought to conclude, not (as is too usual among tasteless readers) that the author wants those perfections which have been admired in him, but that he himself wants the faculty of discovering them.

He should, in the second place, be very careful to observe, whether he tastes the distinguishing perfections, or, if I may be allowed to call them so, the specific qualities of the author whom he peruses; whether he is particularly pleased with Livy for his manner of telling a story; with Sallust, for his entering into those internal principles of action which arise from the characters and manners of the persons he describes; or with Tacitus, for his displaying those outward motives of safety and interest, which give birth to the whole series of transactions which he relates.

He may likewise consider how differently he is affected by the same thought which presents itself in a great writer, from what he is when he finds it delivered by a person of an ordinary genius. For there is as much difference in apprehending a thought clothed in Cicero's language, and that of a common author, as in seeing an object by the light of a taper, or by the light of the sun.

It is very difficult to lay down rules for the acquirement of such a taste as that I am here speaking of. The faculty must in some degree be born with us, and it very often happens that those, who have other qualities in perfection are wholly void of this. One of the most eminent mathematicians of the age has assured me, that the greatest pleasure he took in reading Virgil, was' in examining Æneas's voyage by the map; as I question not but many a modern compiler of history would be delighted with little more in that divine author, than in the bare matters of fact.

But notwithstanding this faculty must in some measure be born with us, there are several methods for cultivating and improving it, and without which it will be very uncertain, and of very little use to the person that possesses it. The most natural method for this purpose is to be conversant among the writings of the most polite authors. A man who has any relish for fine writing either discovers new beauties, or receives stronger impressions from the masterly strokes of a great author every time he peruses him; besides that he naturally wears himself into the same manner of speaking and thinking.

Conversation with men of a polite genius is another method for improving our natural taste. It is impossible for a man of the greatest parts to consider anything in its whole extent, and in all its variety of lights. Every man, besides those general observations which are to be made upon an author, forms several reflexions that are peculiar to his own manner of thinking; so that conversation will naturally furnish us with hints which we did not attend to, and make us enjoy other men's parts and reflexions as well as our own. This is the best reason I can give for the observation which several have made, that men of great genius in the same way of writing seldom rise up singly, but at certain periods of time appear together, and in a body, as they did at Rome in the reign of Augustus, and in Greece about the age of Socrates. I cannot think that Corneille, Racine, Moliére, Boileau, la Fontaine, Bruyère, Bossu, or the Daciers, would have written so well as they have done, had they not been friends and contemporaries.

It is likewise necessary for a man, who would form to himself a finished taste of good writing to be well-versed in the works of the best critics, both ancient and modern. I must confess that I could wish there were authors of this kind, who, besides the mechanical rules, which a man of very little taste may discourse upon, would enter into the very spirit and soul of fine writing, and shew us the several sources of that pleasure which rises in the mind upon the perusal of a noble work. Thus, although in poetry it be absolutely necessary that the unities of time, place, and action, with other points of the same nature, should be thoroughly explained and understood,—there is still something more essential to the art, something that elevates and astonishes the fancy, and gives a greatness of mind to the reader, which few of the critics besides Longinus have considered.

[No. 409. *The Spectator*.]

(*b*) *Pastoral Poetry* (Steele)

Pastoral poetry not only amuses the fancy the most delightfully, but is likewise more indebted to it than any other sort whatsoever. It transports us into a kind of fairy land, where our ears are soothed with the melody of birds, bleating flocks, and purling streams; our eyes enchanted with flowery meadows and springing greens; we are laid under cool shades, and entertained with all the sweets and freshness of nature. It is a dream, it is a vision, which we wish may be real, and we believe that it is true.

. . . In order to form a right judgment of pastoral poetry it will be necessary to cast back our eyes on the first ages of the world. For since that way of life is not now in being, we must inquire into the manner of it when it actually did exist. Before mankind was formed into large societies, or cities were built, and commerce established, the wealth of the world consisted chiefly in flocks and herds. The tending of these, we find to have been the employment of the first princes, whose subjects were sheep and oxen, and their dominions the adjoining vales. As they lived in great affluence and ease, we may presume that they enjoyed such pleasures as that condition afforded, free and uninterrupted. Their manner of life gave them vigour of body, and serenity of mind. The abundance they were possessed of, secured them from avarice, ambition, or envy; they could scarcely have any anxieties or contentions, where everyone had more than he could tell what to do with. Love, indeed, might occasion some rivalships among them, because many lovers fix upon one object, for the loss of which they will be satisfied with no compensation. Otherwise it was a state of ease, innocence, and contentment; where plenty begot pleasure, and pleasure begot singing, and singing begot poetry, and poetry begot pleasure again.

Thus happy was the first race of men, but rude withal, and uncultivated. For before they could make any considerable progress in arts and sciences, the tranquillity of the rural life was destroyed by turbulent and ambitious spirits; who, having built cities, made vassals of the defenceless shepherds, and rendered that which was before easy and unrestrained, a mean, laborious, miserable condition. Hence, if we consider the pastoral period before learning, we shall find it unpolished; if after, we shall find it unpleasant.

The use that I would make of this short review of country life shall be this. An author that would amuse himself by writing pastorals, should form in his fancy a rural scene of perfect ease and tranquillity, where innocence, simplicity, and joy abound. It is not enough, that he writes about the country; he must give us what is agreeable in that scene; and hide what is wretched. It is indeed commonly affirmed, that truth well-painted will please the imagination; but it is sometimes convenient not to discover the whole truth, but that part which only is delightful. We must sometimes shew only half an image to the fancy; which if we display in a lively manner, the mind is so dexterously deluded, that it doth not readily perceive that the other half is concealed. Thus, in writing pastorals, let the tranquillity of that life appear full and plain, but hide the meanness of it; represent its simplicity as clear as you please, but cover its misery. I would not hereby be so understood, as if I thought nothing that is irksome or unpleasant should have a place in these writings: I only mean that this state of life in general should be supposed agreeable. But as there is no condition exempt from anxiety, I will allow shepherds to be afflicted with such misfortunes as the loss of a favourite lamb, or a faithless mistress. He may, if you please, pluck a thorn out of his foot; or vent his grief for losing the prize in dancing; but these being small torments, they recommend that state which only produces such trifling evils. Again, I would not seem so strict in my notions of innocence and simplicity, as to deny the use of a little railing, or the liberty of stealing a kid or a sheep-hook. For these are likewise such petty enormities, that we must think the country happy where these are the greatest transgressions.

When a reader is placed in such a scene as I have described, and introduced into such company as I have chosen, he gives himself up to the pleasing delusion; and since every one doth not know how it comes to pass, I will venture to tell him why he is pleased.

The first reason is, because all mankind love eases. Though ambition and avarice employ most men's thoughts, they are such uneasy habits, that we do not indulge them out of choice, but from some necessity, real or imaginary. We seek happiness, in which ease is the principal ingredient, and the end proposed in our most restless pursuits is tranquillity. We are therefore soothed and delighted with the representation of it, and fancy we partake of the pleasure.

A second reason is our secret approbation of innocence and simplicity. Human nature is not so much depraved, as to hinder us from respecting goodness in others, though we ourselves want it. This is the reason why we are so much charmed with the pretty prattle of children, and even the expressions of pleasure or uneasiness in some part of the brute creation. They are without artifice or malice; and we love truth too well to resist the charms of sincerity.

A third reason is our love of the country. Health, tranquillity, and pleasing objects are the growth of the country; and though men, for the general good of the world, are made to love populous cities, the country hath the greatest share in an uncorrupted heart. When we paint, describe, or any way indulge our fancy, the country is the scene which supplies us with the most lovely images. This state was that wherein God placed Adam when in Paradise; nor could all the fanciful wits of antiquity imagine anything that could administer more exquisite delight in their Elysium.

[No. 22. *The Guardian*.]

(*c*) *Tragi-comedy* (Addison)

The English writers of tragedy are possessed with a notion, that when they represent a virtuous or innocent person in distress, they ought not to leave him till they have delivered him out of his troubles, or made him triumph over his enemies. This error they have been led into by a ridiculous doctrine in modern criticism, that they are obliged to an equal distribution of rewards and punishments, and an impartial execution of poetical justice. Who were the first that established this rule, I know not; but I am sure it has no foundation in nature, in reason, or in the practice of the ancients. We find that good and evil happen alike to all men on this side the grave; and as the principal design of tragedy is to raise commiseration and terror in the minds of the audience, we shall defeat this great end, if we always make virtue and innocence happy and successful. Whatever crosses and disappointments a good man suffers in the body of the tragedy, they will make but small impression on our minds, when we know that in the last act he is to arrive at the end of his wishes and desires. When we see him engaged in the depth of his afflictions, we are apt to comfort ourselves, because we are sure he will find his way out of them, and that his grief, how great so ever it may be at present, will soon terminate in gladness. For this reason the ancient writers of tragedy treated men in their plays, as they are dealt with in the world, by making virtue sometimes happy and sometimes miserable, as they found it in the fable which they made choice of, or as it might affect their audience in the most agreeable manner. Aristotle considers the tragedies that were written in either of these kinds, and observes, that those which ended unhappily had always pleased the people, and carried away the prize in the public disputes of the stage from those that ended happily. Terror and commiseration leave a pleasing anguish in the mind; and fix the audience in such a serious composure of thought, as is much more lasting and delightful than any little transient starts of joy and satisfaction. Accordingly, we find that more of our English tragedies have succeeded, in which the favourites of the audience sink under their calamities, than those in which they recover themselves out of them. The best plays of this kind are, *The Orphan*, *Venice Preserved* [Otway], *Alexander the Great, Theodosius* [Lee], *All for Love* [Dryden], *Oedipus* [Lee and Dryden], *Oroonoko* [Southerne], *Othello, &c. King Lear* is an admirable tragedy of the same kind, as Shakespeare wrote it; but as it is reformed according to the chimerical notion of poetical justice, in my humble opinion it has lost half its beauty. At the same time I must allow, that there are very noble tragedies, which have been framed upon the other plan, and have ended happily; as indeed most of the good tragedies which have been written since the starting of the above-mentioned criticism have taken this turn: as the *Mourning Bride* [Congreve], *Tamerlane, Ulysses* [Rowe], *Phœdra and Hippolitus* [Racine, adapted by Smith], with most of Mr. Dryden's. I must also allow, that many of Shakespeare's, and several of the celebrated tragedies of antiquity, are cast in the same form. I do not therefore dispute against this way of writing tragedies, but against the criticism that would establish this as the only method, and by that means would very much cramp the English tragedy, and perhaps give a wrong bent to the genius of our writers.

The tragi-comedy, which is the product of the English theatre, is one of the most monstrous inventions that ever entered into a poet's thoughts. An author might as well think of weaving the adventures of Æneas and Hudibras into one poem, as of writing such a motley piece of mirth and sorrow. But the absurdity of these performances is so very visible, that I shall not insist upon it.

The same objections which are made to tragi-comedy may in some measure be applied to all tragedies that have a double plot in them; which are likewise more frequent upon the English stage than upon any other; for though the grief of the audience, in such performances, be not changed into another passion, as in tragi-comedies, it is diverted upon another object, which weakens their concern for the principal action, and breaks the tide of sorrow by throwing it into different channels. This inconvenience, however, may in a great measure be cured, if not wholly removed, by the skillful choice of an under plot, which may bear such a near relation to the principal design, as to contribute towards the completion of it, and be concluded by the same catastrophe.

There is also another particular which may be reckoned among the blemishes, or rather the false beauties, of our English tragedy: I mean those particular speeches which are commonly known by the name of *rants*. The warm and passionate parts of a tragedy are always the most taking with the audience; for which reason we often see the players pronouncing, in all the violence of action, several parts of the tragedy which the author writ with great temper, and designed that they should be so acted. I have seen Powell very often raise himself a loud clap by this artifice. The poets that were acquainted with this secret have given frequent occasion for such emotions in the actor, by adding vehemence to words where there was no passion, or inflaming a real passion into fustian. This has both filled the mouths of our heroes with bombast; and given them such sentiments as proceed rather from a swelling than a greatness of mind. Unnatural exclamations, curses, vows, blasphemies, a defiance of mankind, and an outraging of the gods, frequently pass upon the audience for towering thoughts, and have accordingly met with infinite applause.

... As our heroes are generally lovers, their swelling and blustering upon the stage very much recommends them to the fair part of the audience. The ladies are wonderfully pleased to see a man insulting kings, or affronting the gods in one scene, and throwing himself at the feet of his mistress in another. Let him behave himself insolently towards the men and abjectly towards the fair one, and it is ten to one but he proves a favourite of the boxes. [No. 40. *The Spectator*.]

7
Samuel Johnson

Dr. Johnson (1709-1784) belonged to Lichfield by accident of birth, and to London by choice and temperament. Poverty took him from Oxford University to fight a battle against:

"Toil, envy, want, the patron, and the jail."

It was an unfortunate time for a literary adventurer: the age when merit such as his was recognised and rewarded by party heads was a thing of the past; the age when the reading public was large enough to support several geniuses had not yet arrived. In his campaign for fame his early poems, his journal, *The Rambler,* were successful skirmishes. His *Dictionary* (1747-1755) is the nearest approach to a decisive battle, for *The Lives of the Poets* and his edition of *Shakespeare* (1765) were really chases of a retreating enemy. Really, his personality won the fight. Other writers loved and feared him, and delighted to have him as the Grand Cham of Literature, accepting his laws because they were based on his own solidity, sincerity, and sense—and because the Age of Reason was a law-abiding age.

The printed word cannot hold Johnson: he bursts the chains and insists on being alive. The extracts from Boswell's *Life of Dr. Samuel Johnson* and from his *Journal of a Tour to the Hebrides* remind us that the critical mind may find an outlet in the tongue as well as in the pen. Johnson's written criticism, represented by part of his *Preface to Shakespeare,* is as good as it is because he was speaking criticism for so great a part of his adult life.

Like our greatest newspapers, Johnson had bias and limitations, but the lack of deception about the latter and the honesty behind the former contribute a flavour that is part of their appeal. Johnson would not overlook the lack of a moral in serious writing; Cowper was convinced that the Doctor had "no ear for poetical numbers, or that it was stopped by prejudice against the harmony of Milton's"; he was interested in Man, not in Mountains or in Nature as a thing apart; mysticism was beyond his reach; Love meant affection, not passion. We note his imperfections and find they cannot turn the scale against his virtues. Behind ever expression of criticism was the combined force of tremendous reading, an insistence that more was to be learned from life than books, a constant reference to sense and experience as touchstones, a belief that the laws of his age should be founded on the mind of that age, not of an earlier one. He will worship the idol he has set up, but not that of others. When he speaks he is clear, forceful, and masterful. "He makes new things familiar and familiar things new. He tells us what we did not know before with such convincing force and clearness that we embrace it and make it our own. He tells us what we knew already in such a way that we know it as we never knew it before."

(*a*) From Boswell's *Life of Johnson*

"My dear friend, clear your mind of cant. You may *talk* as other people do . . . but don't *think* foolishly."

"Sir, I do not think Gray a first-rate poet. He has not a bold imagination, nor much command of words. The obscurity in which he has involved himself will not persuade us that he is sublime. His Elegy in a church-yard has a happy selection of images."

"Sir, there is all the difference in the world between characters of nature and characters of manners; and *there* is the difference between the characters of Fielding and those of Richardson. Characters of manners are very entertaining; but they are to be understood, by a mere superficial observer, than characters of nature, where a man must dive into the recesses of the human heart."

Talking on the subject of taste in the arts, he said, that difference of taste was, in truth, difference of skill.

Boswell. "But, sir, is there not a quality called taste, which consists merely in perception or in liking? For instance, we find people differ much as to what is the best style of English composition. Some think Swift's the best, others prefer a fuller and a grander style of writing."

Johnson. "Sir, you must first define what you mean by style, before you can judge who has a good taste in style, and who has a bad. The two classes of persons whom you have mentioned don't differ as to good and bad. They both agree that Swift has a good neat style; but one loves a neat style, another likes a style of more splendour. In like manner, one loves a plain coat, another loves a laced coat; but neither will deny that each is good in its kind."

Johnson praised John Bunyan highly. "His *Pilgrim's Progress* has great merit, both' for invention, imagination, and the conduct of the story; and it has had the best evidence of its merit, the general and continued approbation of mankind."

We talked of translation. I said, I could not define it, nor could I think of a similitude to illustrate it; but that it appeared to me the translation of poetry could be only imitation.

Johnson. "You may translate books of science exactly. You may also translate history, in so far as it is not embellished with oratory, which is poetical. Poetry, indeed, cannot be translated; and, therefore, it is the poets that preserve languages; for we would not be at the trouble to learn a language, if we could have all that is written in it just as well in a translation."

"Thomson had a true poetical genius, the power of viewing everything in a poetical light. His fault is such a cloud of words sometimes that the sense can hardly peep through. Shiels . . . was one day sitting with me. I took down Thomson, and read aloud a large portion to him, and then asked,—Is not this fine? Shiels having expressed the highest admiration. Well, sir (said I), I have omitted every other line."

I was somewhat disappointed in finding that the edition of the English Poets, for which he was to write Prefaces and Lives, was not an undertaking directed by him; but that he was to furnish a Preface and Life to any poet the booksellers pleased. I asked him if he would do this to any dunce's works, if they should ask him.

Johnson. "Yes, sir, and *say* he was a dunce."

I mentioned Mallet's tragedy of *Elvira,* . . . and that the Hon. Andrew Erskine, Mr. Dempster and myself, had joined in writing a pamphlet, entitled *Critical Strictures,* against it. That the mildness of Dempster's disposition had, however, relented; and he had candidly said, "We have hardly a right to abuse this tragedy: for bad as it is, how vain should either of us be to write one not near so good."

Johnson. "Why, no, sir; this is not just reasoning. You *may* abuse a tragedy, though you cannot write one. You may scold a carpenter who has made you a bad table, though you cannot make a table. It is not your trade to make tables."

Mrs. Montagu, a lady distinguished for having written an Essay on Shakespeare, being mentioned:

Reynolds. "I think that essay does her honour."

Johnson. "Yes, sir, it does *her* honour, but it would do nobody else honour. I have, indeed, not read it all. But when I take up the end of a web, and find it packthread, I do not expect, by looking further, to find embroidery. Sir, I will venture to say, there is not one sentence of true criticism in her book."

Garrick. "But, sir, surely it shows how much Voltaire has mistaken Shakespeare, which nobody else has done."

Johnson. "Sir, nobody else has thought it worthwhile. And what merit is there in that? You may as well praise a schoolmaster for whipping a boy, who has construed ill. No, sir, there is no real criticism in it: none shewing the beauty of thought, as formed on the workings of the human heart. . . . We have an example of true criticism in Burke's *Essay on the Sublime and the Beautiful.* . . . There is no great merit in telling how many plays have Ghosts in them, and how this Ghost is better than that. You must show how terror is impressed on the human heart."

(*b*) From the *Journal of a Tour to the Hebrides*

Johnson. "... now learning is in itself a trade. A man goes to a bookseller and gets what he can. We have done with patronage.

In the infancy of learning, we find some great man praised for it. This diffused it among others. When it becomes general, an author leaves the great, and applies to the multitude."

Boswell. "It is a shame that authors are not now better patronized."

Johnson. "No, sir. If learning cannot support a man, if he must sit with his hands across till somebody feeds him, it is as to him a bad thing, and it is better as it is. While a man is *in equilibrio,* he throws truth among the multitude, and lets them take it as they please; in patronage, he must say what pleases his patron, and it is an equal chance whether that be truth or falsehood."

Watson. "But is it not the case now, that, instead of flattering one person, we flatter the age?"

Johnson. "No, sir. The world always lets a man tell what he thinks, his own way."

(*c*) From the *Preface to Shakespeare*

Nothing can please many, and please long, but just representations of general nature. . . . The mind can only repose on the stability of truth.

Shakespeare is above all writers, at least above all modern writers, the poet of nature; the poet that holds up to his readers a faithful mirror of manners and of life. His characters are not modified by the customs of particular places, unpractised by the rest of the world; by the peculiarities of studies or professions, which can operate but upon small numbers; or by the accidents of transient fashions or temporary opinions: they are the genuine progeny of common humanity, such as the world will always supply, and observation will always find. His persons act and speak by the influence of those general passions and principles by which all minds are agitated, and the whole system of life is continued in motion. In the writings of other poets a character is too often an individual; in those of *Shakespeare* it is commonly a species.

. . . The theatre, when it is under any other direction, is peopled by such characters as were never seen, conversing in a language which was never heard, upon topics which will never arise in the commerce of mankind. But the dialogue of this author is often so evidently determined by the incident which produces it, and is pursued with so much ease and simplicity, that it seems scarcely to claim the merit of fiction, but to have been gleaned by diligent selection out of common conversation, and common occurrences.

Upon every other stage the universal agent is love, by whose power all good and evil is distributed, and every action quickened or retarded. To bring a lover, a lady and a rival into the fable; to entangle them in contradictory obligations, perplex them with violence of desires inconsistent with each other; to make them meet in rapture and part in agony; to fill their mouths with hyperbolical joy and outrageous sorrow; to distress them as nothing human ever was distressed; to deliver them as nothing human ever was delivered; is the business of a modern dramatist. For this probability is violated, life is misrepresented, and language is depraved. But love is only one of many passions; and as it has no great influence upon the sum of life, it has little operation in the dramas of a poet, who caught his ideas from the living world, and exhibited only what he saw before him. He knew, that any other passion, as it was regular or exorbitant, was a cause of happiness or calamity.

. . . Other dramatists can only gain attention by hyperbolical or aggravated characters, by fabulous and unexampled excellence or depravity, as the writers of barbarous romances invigorated the reader by a giant and a dwarf; and he that should form his expectations of human affairs from the play, or from a tale, would be equally deceived. *Shakespeare* has no heroes; his scenes are occupied only by men, who act and speak as the reader thinks that he should himself have spoken or acted on the same occasion. Even where the agency is supernatural the dialogue is level with life. Other writers disguise the most natural passions and most frequent incidents; so that he who contemplates them in the book will not know them in the world: *Shakespeare* approximates the remote, and familiarizes the wonderful; the event which he represents will not happen, but if it were possible, its effects would probably be such as he has assigned; and it may be said, that he has not only shewn human nature as it acts in real exigencies, but as it would be found in trials, to which it cannot be exposed.

Notes are often necessary, but they are necessary evils. Let him, that is yet unacquainted with the powers of *Shakespeare*, and who desires to feel the highest pleasure that the drama can give, read every play from the first scene to the last, with utter negligence of all his commentators. When his fancy is once on the wing, let it not stop at correction or explanation. When his attention is strongly engaged, let it disdain alike to turn aside to the name of *Theobald* and of *Pope*. Let him read on through brightness and obscurity, through integrity and corruption; let him preserve his comprehension of the dialogue and his interest in the fable. And when the pleasures of novelty have ceased, let him attempt exactness, and read the commentators.

. . . Parts are not to be examined till the whole has been surveyed; there is a kind of intellectual remoteness necessary for the comprehension of any great work in its full design and its true proportions; a close approach shews the smaller niceties, but the beauty of the whole is discerned no longer.

8

Hazlitt

William Hazlitt (1778-1830) was born with a double share of enthusiasm, which found its chief outlet in Coleridge (whom he met in 1798), Napoleon (whom he admired to the end), Shakespeare, and good writing of all ages. By nature unfitted for domesticity, he created his own circle and lived in it abundantly. More of a thinker than a reader, he had the ability to feel the spirit of a book and to express his enthusiasm infectiously. His contributions to the enjoyment and appreciation of literature included *Characters of Shakespeare's Plays* (1817), important because "He really understood that Shakespeare was a dramatic craftsman"; *Lectures on the English Poets* (1819), which showed he appreciated the value of ages that it was then fashionable to misrepresent and belittle; *The Spirit of the Age* (1825), in which he mistook fewer geese for swans than criticism of contemporary poetry usually does, and led the age to see the merits of the new school of Poetry. But criticism creeps into all his writing: in *Table Talk* (from which our essay is taken) and *Winterslow Papers* we have, besides the best of his essays, many expressions of his brilliant critical mind. He was as forthright as Dr. Johnson; in his own way a lighter gun but equally accurate in aim

On Familiar Style

It is not easy to write a familiar style. Many people mistake a familiar for a vulgar style, and suppose that to write without affectation is to write at random. On the contrary, there is nothing that requires more precision, and, if I may so say, purity of expression, than the style I am speaking of. It utterly rejects not only all unmeaning pomp, but all low, cant phrases, and loose, unconnected, *slipshod* allusions. It is not to take the first word that offers, but the best word in common uses; it is not to throw words together in any combinations we please, but to follow and avail ourselves of the true idiom of the language. To write a genuine familiar or truly English style, is to write as anyone would speak in common conversation, who had a thorough command and choice of words, or who could discourse with ease, force, and perspicuity, setting aside all pedantic and oratorical flourishes. Or to give another illustration, to write naturally is the same thing in regard to common conversation, as to read naturally is in regard to common speech. It does not follow that it is an easy thing to give the true accent and inflection to the words you utter, because you do not attempt to rise above the level of ordinary life and colloquial speaking. You do not assume indeed the solemnity of the pulpit, or the tone of stage-declamation: neither are you at liberty to gabble on at a venture, without emphasis or discretion, or to resort to vulgar dialect or clownish pronunciation. *You must steer a middle course.* You are tied down to a given and appropriate articulation, which is determined by the habitual associations between sense and sound, and which you can only hit by entering into the author's meaning, as you must find the proper words and style to express yourself by fixing your thoughts on the subject you have to write about. Anyone may mouth out a passage with a theatrical cadence or get upon stilts to tell his thoughts: but to write or speak with propriety and simplicity is a more difficult task. Thus, it is easy to affect a pompous style, to use a word twice as big as the thing you want to express: it is not so easy to pitch upon the very word that exactly fits it. Out of eight or ten words equally common, equally intelligible, with nearly equal pretensions, it is a matter of some nicety and discrimination to pick out the very one, the preferableness of which is scarcely perceptible, but decisive. The reason why I object to Dr. Johnson's style is, that there is no discrimination, no selection, no variety in it. He uses none but "tall, opaque words," taken from the "first row of the rubric"—words with the greatest number of syllables, or Latin phrases with merely English terminations. If a fine style depended on this sort of arbitrary pretension, it would be fair to judge of an author's elegance by the measurement of his words, and the substitution of foreign circumlocutions (with no precise associations) for the mother-tongue. [I have heard of such a thing as an author, who makes it a rule never to admit a monosyllable into his vapid verse. Yet the charm and sweetness of Marlow's lines depended often on their being made up almost entirely of monosyllables.] How simple it is to be dignified without ease, to be pompous without meaning! Surely, it is but a mechanical rule for avoiding what is low to be always pedantic and affected. It is clear you cannot use a vulgar English word, if you never use a common English word at all. A fine tact is shown in adhering to those which are perfectly common, and yet never falling into any expressions which are debased by disgusting circumstances, or which owe their signification and point to technical or professional allusions. A truly natural or familiar style can never be quaint or vulgar, for this reason, that it is of universal force and applicability, and that quaintness and vulgarity arise out of the immediate connection of certain words with coarse and disagreeable, or with confined ideas. The last form what we understand by *cant* or *slang* phrases. To give an example of what is not very clear in the general statement. I should say that the phrase *To cut with a knife* or *To cut a piece of wood* is perfectly free from vulgarity, because it is perfectly common: but to *cut an acquaintance* is not quite unexceptionable because it is not perfectly common or intelligible, and has hardly yet escaped out of the limits of slang phraseology. I should hardly therefore use the word in this sense without putting it in italics as a license of expression, to be received *cum grano salis.*[1] All provincial or bye-phrases come under the same mark of reprobation—all such as the writer transfers to his page from his fireside or a particular *coterie,* or that he invents for his own sole use and convenience. I conceive that words are like money, not the worse for being common, but that it is the stamp of custom alone that gives them circulation or value. I am fastidious in that respect, and would almost as soon coin the currency of the realm as counterfeit the King's English. I never invented or gave a new and unauthorised meaning to any word but one single one (the term *impersonal* applied to feelings) and that was in an abstruse metaphysical discussion to express a very difficult distinction. I have been (I know) loudly accused of revelling in vulgarisms and broken English. I cannot speak to that point: but so far I plead guilty to the determined use of acknowledged idioms and common elliptical expressions. I am not sure that the critics in question know the one from the other, that is, can distinguish any medium between formal pedantry and the most barbarous solecism. As an author, I endeavour to employ plain words and popular modes of construction, as were I a Chapman and dealer, I should common weights and measures.

The proper force of words lies not in the words themselves, but in their application. A word may be a fine-sounding word, of an unusual length, and very imposing from its learning and novelty, and yet in the connection, in which it is introduced, may be quite pointless and irrelevant. It is not pomp or pretension, but the adaptation of the expression to the idea that clenches a writer's meaning:—as it is not the size or glossiness of the materials, but their being fitted each to its place, that gives strength to the arch; or as the pegs and nails are as necessary to the support of the building as the larger timbers, and more so than the mere showy, unsubstantial ornaments. I hate anything that occupies more space than it is worth. I hate to see a load of band-boxes go along the street, and I hate to see a parcel of big words without anything in them. A person who does not deliberately dispose of all his thoughts alike in cumbrous draperies and flimsy disguises, may strike out twenty varieties of familiar everyday language, each coming somewhat nearer to the feeling he wants to convey, and at last not hit upon that particular and only one, which may be said to be identical with the exact impression in his mind. This would seem to show that Mr. Cobbett[2] is hardly right in saying that the first word that occurs is always the best. It may be a very good one; and yet a better may present itself on reflection or from time to time. It should be suggested naturally, however, and spontaneously, from a fresh and lively conception of the subject. We seldom succeed by trying at improvement, or by merely substituting one word for another that we are not satisfied with, as we cannot recollect the name of a place or person by merely plaguing ourselves about it. We wander farther from the point by persisting in a wrong scent; but it starts up accidentally in the memory when we least expected it, by touching some link in the chain of previous association.

There are those who hoard up and make a cautious display of nothing but rich and rare phraseology ancient medals, obscure coins, and Spanish pieces of eight. They are very curious to inspect; but I would myself neither offer nor take them in the course of exchange. A sprinkling of archaisms is not amiss; but a tissue of obsolete expressions is more fit *for keep than wear.* I do not say I would not use any phrase that had been brought into fashion before the middle or the end of the last century; but I should be shy of using any that had not been employed by any approved author during the whole of that time. Words, like clothes, get old-fashioned, or mean and ridiculous, when they have been for some time laid aside. Mr. Lamb is the only imitator of old English style I can read with pleasure; and he is so thoroughly imbued with the spirit of his authors, that the idea of imitation is almost done away. There is an inward punction, a marrowy vein, both in the thought and feeling, an intuition, deep and lively, of his subject, that carries off any quaintness or awkwardness arising from an antiquated style and dress. The matter is completely his own, though the manner is assumed. Perhaps his ideas are altogether so marked and individual, as to require their point and pungency to be neutralised by the affectation of a singular but traditional form of conveyance. Tricked out in the prevailing costume, they would probably seem more startling and out of the way. The old English authors, Burton,[3] Fuller,[4] Coryate,[5] Sir Thomas Browne,[6] are a kind of mediators between us and the more eccentric and whimsical modern, reconciling us to his peculiarities. I do not however know how far this is the case or not, till he condescends to write like one of us. I must confess that what I like best of his papers under the signature of "Elia" (still I do not presume, amidst such excellence, to decide what is most excellent) is the account of "Mrs. Battle's Opinions on Whist," which is also the most free from obsolete allusions and turns of expression—

"A well of native English undefiled."

To those acquainted with his admired prototypes, these Essays of the ingenious and highly gifted author have the same sort of charm and relish, that Erasmus's *Colloquies*[7] or a fine piece of modern Latin have to the classical scholar. Certainly, I do not know any borrowed pencil that has more power or felicity of execution than the one of which I have here been speaking.

It is as easy to write a gaudy style without ideas, as it is to spread a pallet of showy colours, or to smear in a flaunting transparency. "What do you read?"—"Words, words, words."—"What is the matter?" —" *Nothing,*" it might be answered. The florid style is the reverse of the familiar. The last is employed as an unvarnished medium to convey ideas; the first is resorted to as a spangled veil to conceal the want of them. When there is nothing to be set down but words, it costs little to have them fine. Look through the dictionary, and cull out a *florilegium*,[8] rival the *tulippomania*.[9] *Rouge* high enough, and never mind the natural complexion. The vulgar, who are not in the secret, will admire the look of preternatural health and vigour; and the fashionable, who regard only appearances, will be delighted with the imposition. Keep to your sounding generalities, your tinkling phrases, and all will be well. Swell out an unmeaning truism to a perfect *tympany*[10] of style. A thought, a distinction, is the rock on which all this brittle cargo of verbiage splits at once. Such writers have merely *verbal* imaginations that retain nothing but words. Or their puny thoughts have dragon-wings, all green and gold. They soar far above the vulgar failing of the *sermo humi obrepens*[11]— their most ordinary speech is never short of an hyper-bole, splendid, imposing, vague, incomprehensible, *magniloquent*, a *cento*[12] of sounding common-places. If some of us, whose "ambition is more lowly," ply a little too narrowly into nooks and corners to pick up a number of "unconsidered trifles," they never once direct their eyes or lift their heads to seize on any but the most gorgeous, tarnished, thread bare, patch-work set of phrases, the left-off finery of poetic extravagance, transmitted down through successive generations of barren pretenders. If they criticise actors and actresses, a huddled, phantasmagoria of feathers, spangles, floods of light, and oceans of sound float before their morbid sense, which they paint in the style of Ancient Pistol. Not a glimpse can you get of the merits or defects of the performers: they are hidden in a profusion of barbarous epithets and willful rodomontade. Our hypercritics are not thinking of these little *fantoccini*[13] beings—

"That strut and fret their hour upon the stage,"

but of tall phantoms of words, abstractions, *genera* and *species,* sweeping clauses, periods that unite the Poles, forced alliterations, astounding antitheses—

"And on their pens *Fustian* sits plumed."

[1]*cum grano satis*—" with a pinch of salt."

[2]*Mr. Cobbett*—author of *Rural Rides.*

[3]*Burton, Robert* (1577-1640), author of *The Anatomy of Melancholy.*

[4]*Fuller, Thomas* (1608-1661), theologian and antiquary.

[5]*Coryate, Thomas* (1577-1617), traveller, author of *Coryate's Crudities.*

[6]*Sir Thomas Browne* (1605-1682), artist in prose, author of *Religio Medici* and *Urn Burial.*

[7]*Erasmus's Colloquies,* dialogues for the young scholar, containing humour and satire.

[8]*florilegium*—"a gathering of flowers," an anthology.

[9]*tulippomania*—"craze for tulips" (as in *The Black Tulip).*

[10]*tympany*—"tightness of a drum skin."

[11]*sermo humi obrepens*—" speech of crawling man."

[12]*cento*—patchwork of lines from varied authors.

[13]*fantoccini*—puppets, marionettes.

9
Lamb

Charles Lamb (1775-1834) defies all the obstacles his mistaken friends place in our path. From *Tales from Shakespeare* (1807) we usually proceed to *Essays of Elia* (1820-1833), and then hear the sad story of the life of "Poor Lamb." If we are not so foolish as to accept him as "a contemporary of Wordsworth and of Keats who liked roast-pig, puns, dog's-eared books, whist, artificial language, writing for magazines, quotations, and parodies; who disliked churches, Goethe, the Lake District, philosophy, punctuality, Shelley's voice, sanity, Scots, Jews, and schoolmasters," we come to understand how and why his contemporaries loved the man who hides in the Essays and lives in his Letters. Then we agree with '*The Times*' obituary of 1834: "He was decidedly a man of genius, abounding with original thoughts, and not less remarkable for his power of moving the heart than of amusing the fancy." In 1934 his centenary brought the tribute: "Prose was his art . . . as critic, as essayist, as letter-writer, his claim to the highest rank cannot be seriously contested."

Lamb was true to himself and never followed a fashion. He dared to praise Skelton, Donne, and Dryden when it was unfashionable. Usually his judgments on older literature were sound even when, as with his praise of Elizabethan dramatists, his enthusiasm was unbounded. Portraits of actors like Dicky Suett, essays such as *My First Play,* all show his delight in the theatre.

We give the most important part of his Essay of 1811, "On the Tragedies of Shakespeare, considered with reference to their fitness for stage representation." The stimulus was a section of Garrick's epitaph which dared to hint that the actor was as much a genius as was Shakespeare. Lamb thought that it was difficult for a writer to create a great character, and comparatively easy for an actor to express that character by means of "those low tricks upon the eye and ear." After admitting how hard it is to separate the actor from the part (as we to-day confuse Mr. Gielgud with Mr. Gielgud's Hamlet), he expresses his delight in two actors' interpretations of Shakespeare's characters. The price, he thinks, is too high: "instead of realizing an idea" [the picture created in the reader's mind] "we have only materialized and brought down a fine vision to the standard of flesh and blood." He is fighting in defence of the reader's personal conceptions. Hence, he enjoys the most those plays which he has not seen performed.

On the Tragedies of Shakespeare

It may seem a paradox, but I cannot help being of opinion that the plays of Shakespeare are less calculated for performance on a stage, than those of almost any other dramatist whatever. Their distinguished excellence is a reason that they should be so. There is so much in them, which comes not under the province of acting, with which eye, and tone, and gesture have nothing to do.

The glory of the scenic art is to personate passion, and the turns of passion; and the more coarse and palpable the passion is, the more hold upon the eyes and ears of the spectators the performer obviously possesses. . . . But in all the best dramas, and in Shakespeare above all, how obvious it is, that the form of *speaking,* whether it be in soliloquy or dialogue, is only a medium, and often a highly artificial one, for putting the reader or spectator into possession of that inner knowledge of the inner structure and workings of a mind in a character, which he could otherwise never have arrived at *in that form of composition* by any gift short of intuition.

. . . But the practice of stage representation reduces everything to a controversy of elocution. Every character, from the boisterous blaspheming of Bajazet to the shrinking timidity of womanhood, must play the orator. The love-dialogues of Romeo and Juliet, those silver-sweet sounds of lovers' tongues by night; the more intimate and sacred sweetness of nuptial colloquy between an Othello or a Posthumous with their married wives, all those delicacies which are so delightful in the reading, as when we read of those youthful dalliances in Paradise—

"As beseem'd
Fair couple link'd in happy nuptial league
Alone:"

by the inherent fault of stage representation, how are these things sullied and turned from their very nature by being exposed to a large assembly; when such speeches as Imogen addresses to her lord, come drawling out of the mouth of a hired actress, whose courtship, though nominally addressed to the personated Posthumous is manifestly aimed at the spectators, who are to judge of her endearments and her returns of love.

The character of Hamlet is perhaps that by which, since the days of Betterton, a succession of popular performers have had the greatest ambition to distinguish themselves. The length of the part may be one of their reasons. But for the character itself, we find it in a play, and therefore we judge it a fit subject of dramatic representation. The play itself abounds in maxims and reflections beyond any other, and therefore we consider it as a proper vehicle for conveying moral instruction. But Hamlet himself—what does he suffer meanwhile by being dragged forth as a public schoolmaster, to give lectures to the crowd! Why, nine parts in ten of what Hamlet does, are transactions between himself and his moral sense, they are the effusions of his solitary musings, which he retires to holes and corners and the most sequestered parts of the palace to pour forth; or rather, they are the silent meditations with which his bosom is bursting, reduced to *words* for the sake of the reader, who must else remain ignorant of what is passing there. These profound sorrows, these light-and-noise-abhorring ruminations, which the tongue scarce dares utter to deaf walls and chambers, how can they be represented by a gesticulating actor, who comes and mouths them out before an audience, making four hundred people his confidants at once? I say not that it is the fault of the actor so to do; he must pronounce them *ore rotundo,* he must accompany them with his eye, he must insinuate them into his auditory by some trick of eye, tone, or gesture, or he fails. *He must be thinking all the while of his appearance, because he knows that all the while the spectators are judging of it.* And this is the way to represent the shy, negligent, retiring Hamlet.

It is true that there is no other mode of conveying a vast quantity of thought and feeling to a great portion of the audience, who otherwise would never earn it for themselves by reading, and the intellectual acquisition gained this way may, for aught I know, be inestimable; but I am not arguing that Hamlet should not be acted, but how much Hamlet is made another thing by being acted. I have heard much of the wonders which Garrick performed in this part; but as I never saw him, I must have leave to doubt whether the representation of such a character came within the province of his art. Those who tell me of him, speak of his eye, of the magic of his eye, and of his commanding voice: physical properties, vastly desirable in an actor, and without which he can never insinuate meaning into an auditory, —but what have they to do with Hamlet? What have they to do with intellect? In fact, the things aimed at in theatrical representation, are to arrest the spectator's eye upon the form and the gesture, and so to gain a more favourable hearing to what is spoken: it is not what the character is, but how he looks; not what he says, but how he speaks it.

. . . It is common for people to talk of Shakespeare's plays being so *natural*; that everybody can understand him. They are natural indeed, they are grounded deep in nature, so deep that the depth of them lies out of the reach of the most of us.

. . . Of the texture of Othello's mind, the inward construction marvellously laid open with all its strengths and weaknesses, its heroic confidences and its human misgivings, its agonies of hate springing from the depths of love, they [ordinary playgoers] see no more than the spectators at a cheaper rate, who pay their pennies a-piece to look through the man's telescope in Leicester-fields, see into the inward plot and topography of the moon. Some dim thing or other they see, they see an actor personating a passion, of grief, or anger, for instance, and they recognize it as a copy of the usual external effects of such passions; for at least as being true to *that symbol of the emotion which passes current at the theatre for it,* for it is often no more than that: but of the grounds of the passion, its correspondence to a great or heroic nature, which is the only worthy object of tragedy,—that common auditors know anything of this, or can have any such notions dinned into them by the mere strength of an actor's lungs,—that apprehensions foreign to them should be thus infused into them by storm, I can neither believe, nor understand how it can be possible.

. . . I am almost disposed to deny to Garrick the merit of being an admirer of Shakespeare. A true lover of his excellences he certainly was not; for would any true lover of them have admitted into his matchless scenes such ribald trash as Tate and Cibber, and the rest of them, that

"With their darkness durst affront his light,"

have foisted into the acting plays of Shakespeare? I believe it impossible that he could have had a proper reverence for Shakespeare, and have condescended to go through that interpolated scene in *Richard the Third,* in which Richard tries to break his wife's heart by telling her he loves another woman, and says, "if she survives this she is immortal." Yet I doubt not he delivered this vulgar stuff with as much anxiety of emphasis as any of the genuine parts; and for acting, it is as well-calculated as any. But we have seen the part of Richard lately produce great fame to an actor by his manner of playing it, and it lets us into the secret of acting, and of popular judgments of Shakespeare derived from acting. Not one of the spectators, who have witnessed Mr. C.'s exertions in that part, but has come away with a proper conviction that Richard is a very wicked man, and kills little children in their beds, with something like the pleasure which the giants and ogres in children's books are represented to have taken in that practice; moreover, that he is very close and shrewd and devilish cunning, for you could see that by his eye.

But is in fact this the impression we have in reading the Richard of Shakespeare? Do we feel anything like disgust, as we do at that butcher-like representation of him that passes for him on the stage? A horror at his crimes blends with the effect which we feel, but how is it qualified, how is it carried off, by the rich intellect which he displays, his resources, his wit, his buoyant spirits, his vast knowledge and insight into characters, the poetry of his part,—not an atom of all which is made perceivable in Mr. C.'s way of acting it. Nothing but his crimes, his actions, is visible; they are prominent and staring; the murderer stands out, but where is the lofty genius, the man of vast capacity,—the profound, the witty, accomplished Richard?

The truth is, the Characters of Shakespeare are so much the objects of meditation rather than of interest or curiosity as to their actions, that while we are reading any of his great criminal characters,—Macbeth, Richard, even Iago,—we think not so much of the crimes which they commit, as of the ambition, the aspiring spirit, the intellectual activity, which prompts them to overleap those moral fences. ... In Shakespeare so little do the actions comparatively affect us, that while the impulses, the inner mind in all its perverted greatness, solely seems real and is exclusively attended to, the crime is comparatively nothing. But when we see these acts represented, the acts which they do are comparatively everything, their impulses nothing. The state of sublime emotion into which we are elevated by those images of night and horror which Macbeth is made to utter, that solemn prelude with which he entertains the time till the bell shall strike which is to call him to murder Duncan,—when we no longer read it in a book, when we have given up that vantage-ground of abstraction which reading possesses over seeing, and come to see a man in his bodily shape before our eyes actually preparing to commit a murder, if the acting be true and impressive, as I have witnessed it in Mr. K.'s performance of that part, the painful anxiety about the act, the natural longing to prevent it while it yet seems unperpetrated, the too close pressing semblance of reality, give a pain and an uneasiness which totally destroy all the delight which the words in the book convey, where the deed doing never presses upon us with the painful sense of presence: it rather seems to belong to history,—to something past and inevitable, if it has anything to do with time at all. The sublime images, the poetry alone, is that which is present to our minds in the reading.

So to see Lear acted—to see an old man tottering about the stage with a walking-stick, turned out of doors by his daughters in a rainy night has nothing in it but what is painful and disgusting. We want to take him into shelter and relieve him. That is all the feeling which the acting of Lear ever produced in me. But the Lear of Shakespeare cannot be acted. The contemptible machinery, by which they mimic the storm which he goes out in, is not more inadequate to represent the horrors of the real elements, than any actor can be to represent Lear: they might more easily propose to personate the Satan of Milton upon a stage, or one of Michael Angelo's terrible figures. The greatness of Lear is not in corporal dimension, but in intellectual: the explosions of his passion are terrible as a volcano: they are storms turning up and disclosing to the bottom that sea, his mind, with all its vast riches. It is his mind which is laid bare. This case of flesh and blood seems too insignificant to be thought on; even as he himself neglects it. On the stage we see nothing but corporal infirmities and weakness, the impotence of rage; while we read it, we see not Lear, but we are Lear,—we are in his mind, we are sustained by a grandeur which baffles the malice of daughters and storms; in the aberrations of his reason, we discover a mighty irregular power of reasoning, immethodized from the ordinary purposes of life, but exerting its powers, as the wind blows where it listeth, at will upon the corruptions and abuses of mankind. What have looks, or tones, to do with that sublime identification of his age with that of the *heavens themselves* when in his reproaches to them for conniving at the injustice of his children, he reminds them that 'they themselves are old'? What gesture shall we appropriate to this? What has the voice or the eye to do with such things? But the play is beyond all art, as the tampering with it show: it is too hard and stony; it must have love-scenes, and a happy ending. It is not enough that Cordelia is a daughter, she must shine as a lover too. Tate has put his hook in the nostrils of this Leviathan, for Garrick and his followers, the showmen of the scene, to draw the mighty beast about more easily. A happy ending!—as if the living martyrdom that Lear had gone through—the flaying of his feelings alive—did not make a fair dismissal from the stage of life the only decorous thing for him.

. . . Lear is essentially impossible to be represented on a stage.

To assess the value of Lamb's attack, these points must be considered:

(i) Lamb had never seen Lear acted.

(ii) Lamb's reverence for Shakespeare was that of a lover of *reading*.

(iii) Shakespeare wrote his plays for the theatre in which he worked. He took no interest in preparing a text for printer and reader. To him a play was something to be acted, not to be read. He knew his actors, his audience, and the peculiarities of his stage.

(iv) It is a mistake to consider Shakespeare's plays apart from the curtainless raised platform that brought the actors and the play into the heart of the audience. Lamb's objection "the elaborate and anxious provision of scenery, which the luxury of the age demands, works a quite contrary effect to what is intended," does not contribute to the question, "Can Shakespeare's plays be acted?" but merely criticises the methods of production of his own day.

(v) Garrick gave Shakespeare an enormous vogue. He did much to restore the purity of the text to the stage. Adulation may have turned his head and caused him to regard Shakespeare as "raw material, to be worked up by anyone who thought himself clever enough." But he gave impetus to a movement to stick to what Shakespeare wrote, even though all interpolations and alterations had not been amended by Lamb's day. In our own day it is rare to see a performance that gives all Shakespeare's words in Shakespeare's order.

(vi) At this time playhouses were becoming larger. This in itself added to the difficulty of interpreting by one technique plays written for another. Moreover, it induced producers to try the lavish and spectacular in order to fill the house. A larger house, with actors farther from the back seats, tended to cause what Lamb called "spouting."

(vii) "The orotund acting of his day, its conventional tricks, can have been but a continual offence to his sensitive ear and nicety of taste. He here takes his revenge—and it is an ample one—for many evenings of such suffering. He never stopped to consider whether there might not be even more to the actor's despised art than that" (Granville-Barker).

(viii) Lamb is no superficial reader. He proves time and again that he has come to know Shakespeare by study. He is really pleading that the reader's vision is the true vision, without conceding that when "Hamlet is made another thing by being acted," the actor, by bringing the reader nearer to the vision of the playwright, who conceived Hamlet in action and not in print, may teach the reader much that he could never guess unless he was by nature and training fitted to reconstruct the printed words in terms of the stage.

(ix) That the producers of one age were too fond of mechanical devices to suggest storm does not prove that a reasonable use is impossible.

10

Wordsworth and Coleridge

William Wordsworth (1770-1850) owed little to school or college, but much to the Lake District which was his home, to the fervent support of the French Revolution that many young men of his day gave whole-heartedly, and possibly most to his friendship with Coleridge from 1795. He was able to devote himself to poetry, and with Coleridge planned and produced *Lyrical Ballads* (1798), which startled and divided the readers of poetry. Wiser critics recognised in it something new and something vital: the novelty of the manner and matter irritated conservative readers. A reply to criticisms was made by Wordsworth in the preface to the second edition (Coleridge's share was "The Ancient Mariner": it was on Wordsworth's share that the attack fell). At intervals in a long life Wordsworth continued to produce poetry of varying merit, and lived to see the high qualities of his best work valued.

Samuel Taylor Coleridge (1772-1834) had a brilliant mind that shed light on many branches of art during his restless career. His reputation as a poet rests chiefly on "The Ancient Mariner," "Christabel," and "Kubla Khan." As a school fellow he impressed Lamb, as a preacher he inspired Hazlitt, as a talker he enthralled every one. Philosophy was his hobby-horse; thinking with illumination and something approaching genius became almost a habit. He left brilliant fragments, notably *Biographia Literaria* (1817)—"that powerful, knowledge-packed, revolutionary, critical, ill-shaped, incomplete book," full of good things and often a Book of Revelations—*Lectures* *on Shakespeare,* and *Table Talk*. Discursive as he could be, fragmentary as many of his writings are, he was one of the principal intellectually formative forces of his time. His strong sympathy, his understanding of the nature of creative genius, his obvious enjoyment of the best, his ability to feel and express the individuality of a writer make his work stimulating and enduring. "On the whole, there is no greater English critic, and there are few greater in the modern world." [O. Elton.]

(*a*)
Wordsworth's Preface to the second edition of *The Lyrical Ballads*

It was published, as an experiment which, I hoped, might be of some use to ascertain how far, by fitting to metrical arrangement a selection of the real language of men in a state of vivid sensation, that sort of pleasure and that quantity of pleasure may be imparted which a Poet may rationally endeavour to impart.

. . . The principal object, then . . . was to choose incidents and situations from common life, and to relate or describe them, throughout, as far as was possible, in a selection of language really used by men, and at the same time, to throw over them a certain colouring of imagination, whereby ordinary things should be presented to the mind in an unusual aspect; and, further, and above all, to make these incidents and situations interesting by tracing in them, truly though not ostentatiously, the primary laws of our nature. . . .

The language of these men [of humble and rustic life] has been adopted (purified indeed from what appear to be its real defects, from all lasting and rational causes of dislike and disgust) because such men hourly communicate with the best objects from which the best part of language is originally derived; and because, from their rank in society and the sameness and narrow circle of their intercourse, being less under the influence of social

their feelings and notions in simple and

ions. . . .

find that personifications of abstract ideas

volumes; and are utterly rejected, as an

evate the style, and raise it above prose. My

purpose was to imitate, and, as far as is possible, to adopt the very language of men; and assuredly such personifications do not make any natural or regular part of that language. . . . I have wished to keep the Reader in the company of flesh and blood, persuaded that by so doing I shall interest him. . . . There will also be found in these volumes little of what is usually called poetic diction; as much pains has been taken to avoid it as is ordinarily taken to produce it. . . . I do not know how to give my Reader a more exact notion of the style in which it was my wish and intention to write, than by informing him that I have at all times endeavoured to look steadily at my subject; consequently, there is, I hope, in these Poems little falsehood of description, and my ideas are expressed in language fitted to their respective importance. Something must have been gained by this practice, as it is friendly to one property of all good poetry, namely, good sense: but it has necessarily cut me off from a large portion of phrases and figures of speech which from father to son have long been regarded as the common inheritance of Poets. I have also thought it expedient to restrict myself still further, having abstained from the use of many expressions, in themselves proper and beautiful, but which have been foolishly repeated by bad Poets, till such feelings of disgust are connected with them as it is scarcely possible by an art of association to overpower.

If in a poem there should be found a series of lines, or even a single line, in which the language, though naturally arranged, and according to the strict laws of metre, does not differ from that of prose, there is a numerous class of critics, who, when they stumble across these prosaisms, as they call them, imagine that they have made a notable discovery, and exult over the Poet as over a man ignorant of his own profession. . . . Not only the language of a large portion of every good poem, even of the most elevated character, must necessarily, except with reference to the metre, in no respect differ from that of good prose, but likewise . . . some of the most interesting parts of the best poems will be found to be strictly the language of prose when prose i[illegible] well-written.

. . . The language of Prose may yet be well-adap[illegible] Poetry. . . . We will go further. It may be safely affirm[illegible] there neither is, nor can be, any *essential* difference between the language of prose and metrical composition.

(*b*)
Coleridge on Wordsworth's Theories

My own differences from certain supposed parts of Mr. Wordsworth's theory ground themselves on the assumption, that his words had been rightly interpreted as purporting that the proper diction for poetry in general consists altogether in a language taken, with due exceptions, from the mouths of men in real life, a language which actually constitutes the natural conversation of men under the influence of natural feelings. My objection is, first, that in any sense this rule is applicable only to certain classes of poetry; secondly, that even to these classes it is not applicable, except in such a sense, as hath never by any one (so far as I know or have read) been denied or doubted; and lastly, that as far as, and in that degree in which it is practicable, it is yet a rule useless, if not injurious, and therefore either need not, or ought not, to be practised.

. . . I object . . . to an equivocation in the use of the word "real." Every man's language varies, according to the extent of his knowledge, the activity of his faculties, and the depth or quickness of his feelings. Every man's language has, first, its individualities; secondly, the common properties of the class to which he belongs; and thirdly, words and phrases of universal use. The language of Hooker, Bacon, Bishop Taylor, and Burke, differs from the common language of the learned class only by the superior number and novelty of the thoughts and relations which they had to convey. The language of Algernon Sidney differs not at all from that which every well-educated gentleman would wish to write, and (with due allowances for the undeliberateness, and less connected train, of thinking natural and proper to conversation) such as he would wish to talk. Neither one nor the other differ half as much from the general language of cultivated society, as the language of Mr. Wordsworth's homeliest composition differs from that of a common peasant. For "real" therefore, we must substitute ordinary, or *lingua communis*. And this . . . is no more to be found in the phraseology of low and rustic life than in that of any other class. Omit the peculiarities of each and the result of course must be common to all. And assuredly the omissions and changes to be made in the language of rustics, before it could be transferred to any species of poem, except the drama or other professed imitation, are at least as numerous and weighty as would be required in adapting to the same purpose the ordinary language of tradesmen and manufacturers.

Neither is the case rendered at all more tenable by the addition of the words "in a state of excitement." For the nature of a man's words, where he is strongly affected by joy, grief, or anger, must necessarily depend on the number and quality of the general truths, conceptions, and images, and of the words expressing them, with which his mind has been previously stored. For the property of passion is not to create, but to set in increased activity. . . .

"There neither is nor can be any essential difference between the language of prose and metrical composition." Such is Mr. Wordsworth's assertion. Now prose itself, at least in all argumentative and consecutive works, differs, and ought to differ, from the language of conversation: even as reading ought to differ from talking. Unless therefore the difference denied be that of the mere words, as materials common to all styles of writing, and not of the style itself in the universally admitted sense of the term, it might be naturally presumed that there must exist a still greater between the ordonnance of poetic composition and that of prose, than is expected to distinguish prose from ordinary conversation.

. . . For the question is not, whether there may not occur in prose an order of words, which would be equally proper in a poem; nor whether there are not beautiful lines and sentences of frequent occurrence in good poems, which would be equally becoming as well as beautiful in good prose; for neither the one nor the other has ever been either denied or doubted by any one. The true question must be, whether there are not modes of expression, a construction, and an order of sentences, which are in their fit and natural place in a serious prose composition, but would be disproportionate and heterogeneous in metrical poetry;

and, *vice versa*, whether in the language of a serious poem there may not be an arrangement both of words and sentences, and a use and selection of (what are called) figures of speech, both as to their kind, their frequency, and their occasions, which on a subject of equal weight would be vicious and alien in correct and manly prose. I contend, that in both cases this unfitness of each for the place of the other frequently will and ought to exist.

And first from the origin of metre. This I would trace to the balance in the mind effected by that spontaneous effort which strives to hold in check the workings of passion. ... As the elements of metre owe their existence to a state of increased excitement, so the metre itself should be accompanied by the natural language of excitement. Secondly, that as these elements is formed into metre artificially, by a voluntary act, with the design and for the purpose of blending delight with the emotion, so the traces of present volition should throughout the metrical language be clearly discernible. . . . It [this union] not only dictates, but of itself tends to produce a more frequent employment of picturesque and vivifying language than would be natural in any other case, in which there did not exist, as there does in the present, a previous and well-understood, though tacit, compact between the poet and the reader, that the latter is entitled to expect, and the former bound to supply, this species and degree of pleasurable excitement. . . .

Secondly, I argue from the effects of metre. As far as metre acts in and for itself, it tends to increase the vivacity and susceptibility both of the general feelings and of the attention. This effect it produces by the continued excitement of surprise, and by the quick reciprocations of curiosity still gratified and still re-excited, which are too slight indeed to be at any moment objects of distinct consciousness, yet become considerable in their aggregate influence. As a medicated atmosphere, or as wine during animated conversation, they act powerfully, though themselves unnoticed. Where, therefore, correspondent food and appropriate matter are not provided for the attention and feelings thus roused there must needs be a disappointment felt; like that of leaping in the dark from the last step of a stair-case, when we had prepared our muscles for a leap of three or four. . . .

Metre in itself is simply a stimulant of the attention, and therefore excites the question: Why is the attention to be stimulated? Now the question cannot be answered by the pleasure of the metre itself: for this we have shown to be conditional, and dependent on the appropriateness of the thoughts and expressions, to which the metrical form is superadded. Neither can I conceive any other answer that can be rationally given, short of this: I write in metre, because I am about to use a language different from that of prose. . . .

What then did he [Wordsworth] mean? I apprehend, that in the clear perception, not unaccompanied with disgust or contempt, of the gaudy affectations of a style which passed current with too many for poetic diction, . . . he narrowed his view for the time; and feeling a justifiable preference for the language of nature and of good sense, even in its humblest and least ornamented forms, he suffered himself to express in terms at once too large and too exclusive, his predilection for a style the most remote possible from the false and showy splendour which he wished to explode.

The praise of uniform adherence to genuine, logical English is undoubtedly his; nay, laying the main emphasis on the word *uniform,* I will dare add that, of all contemporary poets it is *his alone*. . . . To me it will always remain a singular and noticeable fact; that a theory, which would establish his *lingua communis,* not only as the best, but as the only commendable style, should have proceeded from a poet, whose diction, next to that of Shakespeare and Milton, appears to me of all others the most *individualized* and characteristic. . . . In short, were there excluded from Mr. Wordsworth's poetic compositions all that a literal adherence to the theory of his preface *would* exclude, two-thirds at least of the marked beauties of his poetry must be erased.

(*c*)
Beauties of Wordsworth's Poetry (Coleridge)

First, an austere purity of language both grammatically and logically; in short, a perfect appropriateness of the words to the meaning. . . . In poetry, in which every line, every phrase, may pass the ordeal of deliberation and deliberate choice, it is possible, and barely possible, to attain that *ultimatum* which I have ventured to propose as the infallible test of a blameless style; namely, its *untranslatableness* in words of the same language without injury to the meaning. Be it observed, however, that I include in the *meaning* of a word, not only its correspondent object, but likewise all the associations which it recalls. For language is framed to convey not the object alone, but likewise the character, mood, and intentions of the person, who is representing it. . . .

The second characteristic excellence of Mr. Wordsworth's work is: a corresponding weight and sanity of the Thoughts and Sentiments,—won, not from books: but—from the poet's own meditative observation. They are *fresh* and have the dew upon them. His muse, at least when in her strength of wing, and when she hovers aloft in her proper element—

"Makes audible a linked lay of truth.
Of truth profound—a sweet continuous lay,
Not learnt, but native, her own natural notes!"

Even throughout his smaller poems there is scarcely one which is not rendered valuable by some just and original reflection. See . . . the last stanza of the poem on the withered Celandine:

"To be a Prodigal's Favorite—then, worse truth,
A Miser's Pensioner—behold our lot!
O Man! that from thy fair and shining youth
Age might but take the things Youth needed not."

If Mr. Wordsworth is not, equally with Daniel, intelligible to all readers of average understanding in all passages of his works, the comparative difficulty does not arise from the greater impurity of the ore, but from the nature and uses of the metal. A poem is not necessarily obscure, because it does not aim to be popular. It is enough, if a work be perspicuous to those for whom it is written, and

"Fit audience find, though few."

Third (and wherein he soars far above Daniel), the sinewy strength and originality of single lines and paragraphs: the frequent *curiosa felicitas* of his diction. This beauty, and as eminently characteristic of Wordsworth's poetry, his rudest assailants have felt themselves compelled to acknowledge and admire.

Fourth, the perfect truth of nature in his images and descriptions as taken immediately from nature, and proving a long and genial intimacy with the very spirit which gives the physiognomic expression to all the works of nature. Like a green field reflected in a calm and perfectly transparent lake, the image is distinguished from the reality only by its greater softness and lustre. Like the moisture or the polish on a pebble, genius neither distorts nor false-colours its objects; but on the contrary brings out many a vein and many a tint, which escape the eye of common observation, thus raising to the rank of gems what had been often kicked away by the hurrying foot of the traveller on the dusty high-road of custom.

Let me refer to the whole description of skating,. . . especially to the lines;

"So through the darkness and the cold we flew,
And not a voice was idle: with the din
Smitten the precipices rang aloud;
The leafless trees and every icy crag
Tinkled like iron; while the distant hills
Into the tumult sent an alien sound
Of melancholy, not unnoticed, while the stars,
Eastward, were sparkling clear, and in the west
The orange sky of evening died away."

. . . or, the poem to the Cuckoo; or, lastly, to the poem, so completely Wordsworth's, commencing—

"Three years she grew in sun and shower"—

Fifth: a meditative pathos, a union of deep and subtle thought with sensibility; a sympathy with man as man; the sympathy indeed of a contemplator, rather than a fellow-sufferer, or co-mate *(spectator, haud particeps),* but of a contemplator, from whose view no difference of rank conceals the sameness of the nature; no injuries of wind or weather, or toil, or even of ignorance, wholly disguise the human face divine. The superscription and the image of the Creator still remain legible to *him* under the dark lines, with which guilt or calamity had cancelled or cross-barred it. Here the Man and the Poet lose and find themselves in each other, the one as glorified, the latter as substantiated. In this mild and philosophical pathos, Wordsworth appears to me without a compeer. Such as he *is*: so he *writes*. See . . . **The Affliction of Margaret; or, The Mad Mother,** of which I cannot refrain from quoting two of the stanzas, both of them for their pathos, and the former for the fine transition in the two concluding lines of the stanza, so expressive of that deranged state, in which, from the increased sensibility, the sufferer's attention is abruptly drawn off by every trifle, and in the same instant plucked back again by the one despotic thought, bringing home with it, by the blending, *fusing* power of Imagination and Passion, the alien object to which it had been so abruptly diverted, no longer an alien but an ally and an inmate:

"Suck, little babe; oh, suck again!
It cools my blood; it cools my brain;
Thy lips, I feel them, baby! they
Draw from my heart the pain away.
Oh! press me with thy little hand;
It loosens something at my chest:
About that tight and deadly band
I feel thy little fingers prest.
The breeze, I see, is in the tree!
It comes to cool my babe and me.

"Thy father cares not for my breast,
Tis thine, sweet baby, there to rest;
'Tis all thine own!—and if its hue
Be changed, that was so fair to view,
'Tis fair enough for thee, my dove!
My beauty, little child, is flown.
But thou wilt live with me in love;
And what if my poor cheek be brown?
'Tis well for me, thou canst not see
How pale and wan it else would be."

Last, and pre-eminently, I challenge for this poet the gift of Imagination, in the highest and strictest sense of the word. In the play of *fancy,* Wordsworth, to my feelings, is not always graceful, and sometimes recondite. The *likeness* is occasionally too strange, or demands too peculiar a point of view, or is such as appears the creature of pre-determined research, rather than spontaneous presentation. Indeed, his fancy seldom displays itself, as mere and unmodified fancy. But in imaginative power, he stands nearest of all modern writers to Shakespeare and Milton; and yet in a kind perfectly unborrowed and his own. To employ his own words, which are at once an instance and an illustration, he does indeed to all thoughts and to all objects—

"add the gleam,
The light that never was, on sea or land,
The consecration, and the Poet's dream."

I shall select a few examples: The effect of the old man's figure in the poem of **Resolution and Independence:—**

"While he was talking thus, the lonely place,
The Old Man's shape, and speech, all troubled me:
In my mind's eye I seemed to see him pace
About the weary moors continually,
Wandering about alone and silently."

Or . . . the sonnet on the subjugation of Switzerland, or the last ode ["On the Intimations of Immortality"], from which I especially select the two . . . stanzas or paragraphs:

"Our birth is but a sleep and a forgetting". . .

and "O joy! that in our embers . . ."

(*d*)
Coleridge on Poetic Genius

A poem is that species of composition which is opposed to works of science, by proposing for its *immediate* object pleasure, not truth: and from all other species—(having *this* object in common with it)— it is discriminated by proposing to itself such delight from the *whole,* as is compatible with a distinct gratification from each component *part.*

[a *legitimate* poem] . . . it must be one, the parts of which mutually support and explain each other; all in their proportion harmonizing with, and supporting the purpose and known influences of metrical arrangement. The philosophic critics of all ages coincide with the ultimate judgment of all countries, in equally denying the praises of a just poem, on the one hand to a series of striking lines or distiches, each of which, absorbing the whole attention of the reader to itself, becomes disjoined from its context, and forms a separate whole, instead of a harmonizing part; and on the other hand, to an unsustained composition, from which the reader collects rapidly the general result unattracted by the component parts. The reader should be carried forward, not merely or chiefly by the mechanical impulse of curiosity, or by a restless desire to arrive at the final solution; but by the pleasurable activity of mind excited by the attractions of the journey itself.

I have endeavoured to discover what the qualities in a poem are, which may be deemed promises and specific symptoms of poetic power, as distinguished from general talent determined to poetic composition by accidental motives, by an act of the will, rather than by the inspiration of a genial and productive nature. . . . From these ["Venus and Adonis," "Lucrece"—"the earliest works of the greatest genius"] I abstracted the following marks, as characteristics of original poetic genius in general.

1. In the **Venus and Adonis,** the first and most obvious excellence is the perfect sweetness of the versification; its adaptation to the subject; and the power displayed in varying the march of the words without passing into a loftier and more majestic rhythm than was demanded by the thoughts, or permitted by the propriety of preserving a sense of melody predominant. The delight in richness and sweetness of sound, even to a faulty excess, if it be evidently original, and not the result of an easily imitable mechanism, I regard as a highly favourable promise in the compositions of a young man. The man that hath not music in his own soul can never be a genuine poet. Imagery, . . . affecting incidents, just thoughts, interesting personal or domestic feelings, and with these the art of

their combination or intertexture in the form of a poem,—may all by incessant effort be acquired as a trade, by a man of talent and much reading, who has mistaken an intense desire of poetic refutation for a naturally poetic genius; the love of the arbitrary end for a possession of the peculiar means. But the sense of musical delight, with the power of producing it, is a gift of imagination; and this together with the power of reducing multitude into unity of effect, and modifying a series of thoughts by someone predominant thought or feeling, may be cultivated and improved, but can never be learned. It is in these that "*poeta nascitur non fit.*"

2. A second promise of genius is the choice of subjects very remote from the private interests and circumstances of the writer himself. At least I have found, that where the subject is taken immediately from the author's personal sensations and experiences, the excellence of a particular poem is but an equivocal mark, and often a fallacious pledge, of genuine poetic power. ... In the **Venus and Adonis** this proof of poetic power exists even to excess. It is throughout as if a superior spirit more intuitive, more intimately conscious, even than the characters themselves, not only of every outward look and act, but of the flux and reflux of the mind in all its subtlest thoughts and feelings, were placing the whole before our view; himself meanwhile unparticipating in the passions, and actuated only by that pleasurable excitement, which had resulted from the energetic fervour of his own spirit in so vividly exhibiting what it had so accurately and profoundly contemplated. . . . His Venus and Adonis seem at once the characters themselves, and the whole representation of those characters by the most consummate actors. You seem to be told nothing, but to see and hear everything. Hence it is, from the perpetual activity of attention required on the part of the reader, from the rapid flow, the quick change, and the playful nature of the thoughts and images; and above all from the alienation, and, if I may hazard such an expression, the utter *aloofness*

of the poet's own feelings, from those of which he is at once the painter and the analyst;—that though the very subject cannot but detract from the pleasure of a delicate mind, yet never was poem less dangerous on a moral account. . . .

3. It has been before observed that images, however beautiful, though faithfully copied from nature, and as accurately represented in words, do not of themselves characterize the poet. They become proofs of original genius only as far as they are modified by a predominant passion; or by associated thoughts or images awakened by that passion; or when they have the effect of reducing multitude to unity, or succession to an instant; or lastly, when a human and intellectual life is transferred to them from the poet's own spirit,

Which shoots its being through earth, sea and air.

In the two following lines, for instance, there is nothing objectionable, nothing which would preclude them from forming, in their proper place, part of a descriptive poem:

Behold yon row of pines, that shorn and bow'd
Bend from the sea-blast, seen at twilight eve.

But with a small alteration of rhythm, the same words would be equally in their place in a book of topography, or in a descriptive tour. The same image will rise into semblance of poetry if thus conveyed:

Yon row of bleak and visionary pines,
By twilight glimpse discerned, mark! how they flee
From the fierce sea-blast, all their tresses wild
Streaming before them.

I have given this as an illustration, by no means as an instance, of that particular excellence which I had in view, and in which Shakespeare even in his earliest, as in his latest, works surpasses all other poets. It is by this that he still gives a dignity and a passion to the objects which he presents. Unaided by any previous excitement, they burst upon us at once in life and in power:

"Full many a glorious morning have I seen?
Flatter the mountain-tops with sovereign eye."

. . . As of higher worth, so doubtless still more characteristic of poetic genius, does the imagery become, when it moulds and colours itself to the circumstances, passion, or character, present and foremost in the mind. For unrivalled instances of this excellence, the reader's own memory will refer him to the **Lear, Othello,** in short to which not of the "*great, ever living, dead man's* dramatic work"?. . .

4. This last character I shall mention, which would prove indeed but little, except as taken conjointly with the former;—yet without which the former could scarce exist in a high degree, and (even if this were possible) would give promises only of transitory flashes and a meteoric power is depth, and energy of thought. No man was ever yet a great poet, without being at the same time a profound philosopher. For poetry are the blossom and the fragrancy of all human knowledge, human thoughts, human passions, emotions, language. In Shakespeare's poems the creative power and the intellectual energy wrestle as in a war embrace. Each in its excess of strength seems to threaten the extinction of the other. At length in the drama they were reconciled, and fought each with its shield before the breast of the other. . .

Shakespeare, no mere child of nature; no *automaton* of genius; no passive vehicle of inspiration, possessed by the spirit, not possessing it; first studied patiently, meditated deeply, understood minutely, till knowledge, become habitual and intuitive, wedded itself to his habitual feelings, and at length gave birth to that stupendous power, by which he stands alone, with no equal or second in his own class.

11

Keats

John Keats (1795-1821) deserted medicine for poetry, encouraged by Leigh Hunt and others, and fortified by a conviction that in him was the power to write poems that could stand worthily beside the masterpieces of the past. Few people noticed his first volume, while the second, *Endymion* (1818), brought on his head the fulminations and vituperations of hostile quarterlies. He was man enough to accept the attacks bravely, artist enough to set to work to improve. In spite of worries caused by his brother's illness, and by his own ill-health, he devoted himself to his art, and in 1820 offered the world a volume that contained "Lamia," "The Eve of St. Agnes," "Hyperion," his Odes and his best Sonnets. The wiser critics, including Jeffrey, recognised its worth. By this time consumption had gained a hold, and his visit to Italy was too late to save him. Speculation as to what heights he might have reached given longer life is interesting but unsatisfying.

One admires the Keats of the poems, and cherishes the Keats of the letters written to his family and his friends. He wrote in utter sincerity without thought of reaching a larger public. To his correspondents he stated and restated, spontaneously, his deep-rooted convictions about the nature of poetry. Coming as they do from one, who devoted himself to poetry and worshipped Beauty, and from one who wrote poems that are among the best of his or of any age, his beliefs command more than respect. He expresses the ideals of Romantic poetry and much more: he writes with freshness and force of the nature of the creative artist.

His letters remind us that Criticism may be like the grain of mustard seed. Truth may dwell on the pens of letter writers as well as on those who are accepted in their day as prophets or appraisers. What matters is the wisdom and soundness of the thought, not the method of communication. Keats joins a band of poets whose letters are valuable because there the practitioner discusses his art; the lover of poetry places the volume of Keats' letters on his bookshelf beside those of Cowper and Hopkins.

(*a*)

To **B. Bailey,** Nov. 1817.

. . . O I wish I was as certain of the end of all your troubles as that of your momentary start about the authenticity of the Imagination. I am certain of nothing but of the holiness of the Heart's affections and the truth of Imagination—what the imagination seizes as Beauty must be truth—whether it existed before or not —for I have the same Idea of all our Passions as of Love: they are all in their sublime, creative of essential Beauty. In a word, you may know my favourite speculation by my first Book *[Endymion]*. . . . The Imagination may be compared to Adam's dream—he awoke and found it truth. I am the more zealous in this affair, because I have never yet been able to perceive how anything can be known for truth by consequitive reasoning—and yet it must be. Can it be that even the greatest Philosopher ever arrived at his goal without putting aside numerous objections? However it may be, O for a life of Sensations rather than of Thoughts!

(*b*)

To **J. H. Reynolds,** Feb. 1818.

. . . It may be said that we ought to read our contemporaries—that Wordsworth, &c., should have their due from us. But, for the sake of a few fine imaginative or domestic passages, are we to be bullied into a certain Philosophy engendered in the whims of an Egotist?— Every man has his speculations, but every man does not brood and peacock over them till he makes a false coinage and deceives himself. Many a man can travel to the very bourne of Heaven, and yet want confidence to put down his half-seeing. Sancho will invent a Journey heavenward as well as anybody. We hate poetry that has a palpable design upon us—and if we do not agree, seems to put its hand in its breeches pocket. Poetry should be great and unobtrusive, a thing which enters into one's soul, and does not startle or amaze it with itself, but with its subject.—How beautiful are the retired flowers! how would they lose their beauty were they to throng into the highway crying out, "Admire me, I am a violet!—dote upon me, I am a primrose!" . . .

(*c*)

To **J. Taylor**, Feb. 1818.

. . . In Poetry I have a few Axioms, ... 1st. I think Poetry should surprise by a fine excess and not by Singularity—it should strike the Reader as a wording of his own highest thoughts, and appear almost a Remembrance.—2nd. Its touches of beauty should never be halfway, thereby making the Reader breathless instead of content: the rise, the progress, the setting of imagery should be like the Sun come natural, natural to him—shine over him and set soberly although in magnificence, leaving him in the luxury of twilight—but it is easier to think what Poetry should be than to write it — and this leads me to another axiom. That if Poetry comes not as naturally as the Leaves to a tree it had better not come at all. . . .

(*d*)

To **R. Woodhouse**, Oct. 1818.

. . . As to the poetical Character itself (I mean that sort of which, if I am anything, I am a member; that sort distinguished from the Wordsworthian or egotistical sublime; which is a thing *per se* and stands alone) it is not itself—it has no self—it is everything and nothing—It has no character—it enjoys light and shade; it lives in gusto, be it foul or fair, high or low, rich or poor, mean or elevated—It has as much delight in conceiving a Iago as an Imogen. What shocks the virtuous philosopher, delights the chameleon

Poet. It does no harm from its relish of the dark side of things any more than from its taste for the bright one; because they both end in speculation. A Poet is the most unpoetical of anything in existence; because he has no Identity—he is continually [informing] and filling some other Body—The Sun, the Moon, the Sea, and Men and Women, who are creatures of impulse are poetical and have about them an unchangeable attribute—the poet has none; no identity — he is certainly the most unpoetical of all God's Creatures. . . .

12
Arnold

Matthew Arnold (1822-1888), the son of Rugby's Dr. Arnold, appeared as a poet in 1849, as a Professor of Poetry in 1857, and as a critic for the rest of his life. He became a self-appointed missionary, a voice crying out in a nineteenth-century wilderness. Behind his earnestness was a suppressed fear of industrial materialism. He felt his age to be a period of comparative barrenness after the prolific Romantic Age, one in which the critic could prepare the ground before the next surge of poetical activity, which would be much better if his doctrine 'keep your standards high' were followed.

He protested against the idea that the highest thing in poetry was the expression of an individual's impressions: to him "the eternal objects of poetry, among all nations, and at all time" were "human actions." He begged his contemporaries to "conceive of poetry worthily and more highly," to think of it "as capable of higher uses and called to higher destinies," to turn to poetry "to interpret life for us, to console us, to sustain us." Readers of poetry must adopt a high standard and a strict judgment, he insists, by basing their valuations not on personal responses or current overrating, but on a sound sense of the greatest achievements of foreign and classical literatures.

In this way he was fighting Carlyle, who directed his countrymen to the Anglo-Saxon virtues, and Ruskin, who wished to tempt people away from the qualities of antiquity to those of the Middle Ages. This "director-general of the intellectual failings of his own nation" found time, too, to trounce the Philistines of his day with their strictly utilitarian standards "His frontal attack on the vulgar and sullen optimism of Victorian utility may be summed up in the admirable sentence, in which he asked the English what was the use of a train taking them quickly from Islington to Camberwell, if it only took them 'from a dismal and illiberal life in Islington to a dismal and illiberal life in Camberwell'?" He was always an apostle of the culture that "is the minister of the sweetness and light essential to the poetic character."

The English people came to admire, and believe in, this unbending defender of classical standards, so much that he became a nineteenth-century Aristotle. His *Essays in Criticism* (our extract is from the second series) will always find readers, for the pleasure in hearing one speak with authority in dignified though austere English.

Poetry as a Criticism of Life

Long ago, in speaking of Homer, I said that the noble and profound application of ideas to life is the most essential part of poetic greatness. I said that a great poet receives his distinctive character of superiority from his application, under the conditions immutably fixed by the laws of poetic beauty and poetic truth, from his application, I say, to his subject, whatever it may be, of the ideas—

"On man, on nature, and on human life,"

which he has acquired for himself. The line quoted is Wordsworth's own; and his superiority arises from his powerful use, in his best pieces, his powerful application to his subject, of ideas "on man, on nature, and on human life."

Voltaire, with his signal acuteness, most truly remarked that "no nation has treated in poetry moral ideas with more energy and depth than the English nation." And he adds:" There, it seems to me, is the great merit of the English poets."

Voltaire does not mean, by "treating in poetry moral ideas," the composing moral and didactic poems;—that brings us but a very little way in poetry. He means just the same thing as was meant when I spoke above "of the noble and profound application of ideas to life"; and he means the application of these ideas under the conditions fixed for us by the laws of poetic beauty and poetic truth. If it is said that to call these ideas *moral* ideas is to introduce a strong and injurious limitation, I answer that it is to do nothing of the kind, because moral ideas are really so main a part of human life. The question, *how to live,* is itself a moral idea; and it is the question which most interests every man, and with which, in some way or other, he is perpetually occupied. A large sense is of course to be given to the term *moral.* Whatever bears upon the question, "how to live," comes under it.

"Nor love thy life, nor hate; but, what thou liv'st,
Live well; how long or short, permit to heaven."

In those fine lines Milton utters, as everyone at once perceives, a moral idea. Yes, but so too, when Keats consoles the forward-bending lover on the Grecian Urn, the lover arrested and presented in immortal relief by the sculptor's hand before he can kiss, with the line,

"For ever wilt thou love, and she be fair"—

he utters a moral idea. When Shakespeare says that

"We are such stuff
As dreams are made of, and our little life
Is rounded with a sleep,"

he utters a moral idea.

. . . It is important, therefore, to hold fast to this: that poetry is at bottom a criticism of life; that the greatness of a poet lies in his powerful and beautiful application of ideas to life, to the question: How to live? Morals are often treated in a narrow and false fashion; they are bound up with systems of thought and belief which have had their day; they are fallen into the hands of pedants and professional dealers; they grow tiresome to some of us. We find attraction, at times, even in a poetry of revolt against them; in a poetry which might take for its motto Omar Khayyam's words: "Let us make up in the tavern for the time which we have wasted in the mosque." Or we find attractions in a poetry indifferent to them; in a poetry where the contents may be what they will, but where the form is studied and exquisite. We delude ourselves in either case; and the best cure for our delusion is to let our minds rest upon that great and inexhaustible word *life,* until we learn to enter into its meaning. A poetry of revolt against moral ideas is a poetry of revolt against *life*; a poetry of indifference towards moral ideas is a poetry of indifference towards *life.*

13

Hardy

Thomas Hardy (1840-1928), born in Dorset, trained as an architect, is worthily admired as poet and novelist. His varied works include in *The Three Strangers* one of our finest short stories; in *The Dynasts* an epic drama unapproached in the last century; in his verse many poems which attract by their depth of feeling, simplicity, and directness, instead of relying on a happy jingle of pleasant sound or movement; in his novels true comedy (*Under the Greenwood Tree)*, and moving tragedy, as in *The Return of the Native,* in which the Wessex scene becomes an important shaper and mirror of events.

From 1867 to 1871 Hardy's creative work was mainly poetry; from 1871 to 1896 he moved from his 'novels of ingenuity,' through 'romances and fantasies,' to his greatest heights, the novels of character and environment, *Tess, Jude the Obscure.* The storm foolishly arising from that last work made him leave fiction and return to poetry, his last volume, *Winter Words,* appearing in 1928. He had written all his novels before Bennett and Galsworthy had begun: they and all later writers profited by the work of Hardy in making fiction to be regarded as serious art and no Cinderella of creative literature.

Hardy's essay of 1891 is a record of the novelist's claim to be taken seriously, a reminder of the contemporary attitude to realism in fiction, and a statement of permanent principles which have an added interest to us to-day, with James Joyce and his imitators in our midst. In 1891 our English novelists were ready to learn from Zola. Partly under his influence they attempted to widen the scope of the novel, and in so doing met opposition from those who were content with the sentimentalism, refinement, and propriety of Victorian fiction. The same battle was being fought on both sides of the Atlantic. "It is still expected," wrote Henry James, only a few years before 1891, that a novel, being only 'make-believe,' "shall renounce the pretension of attempting really to represent life." He complained of "the moral timidity of the usual English novelist; with his (or her) aversion to face the difficulties with which on every side the treatment of reality bristles." The serious artists in America and England were insisting "that the good health of an art which undertakes so immediately to reproduce life must demand that it be perfectly free" to reproduce "the human spectacle," it's sad side as well as any other, with no important section, sex or any other, marked off as forbidden ground.

The Science of Fiction

Since Art is science with an addition, since some science underlies all Art, there is seemingly no paradox in the use of such a phrase as 'the Science of Fiction.' One concludes it to mean that comprehensive and accurate knowledge of realities which must be sought for, or intuitively possessed, to some extent, before anything deserving the name of an artistic performance in narrative can be produced. The materials of fiction being human nature and circumstances, the science thereof may be dignified by calling it the codified laws of things as they really are. No single pen can treat exhaustively of this. The Science of Fiction is contained in that large work, the cyclopaedia of life.

In no proper sense can the term 'science' be applied to other than this fundamental matter. It can have no part or share in the construction of a story, however recent speculations may have favoured such an application. We may assume with certainty that directly the constructive stage is entered upon, Art—high or low—begins to exist.

The most devoted apostle of realism, the sheerest naturalist, cannot escape, any more than the withered old gossip over her fire, the exercise of Art in his labour or pleasure of telling a tale. Not until he becomes an automatic reproducer of all impressions whatsoever can he be called purely scientific, or even a manufacturer on scientific principles. If in the exercise of his reason he select or omit, with an eye to being more truthful than truth (the just aim of Art) he transforms himself into a technicist at a move.

As this theory of the need for the exercise of the Dædalian faculty for selection and cunning manipulation has been disputed, it may be worthwhile to examine the contrary proposition. That it should ever have been maintained by such a romancer as M. Zola, in his work on the *Roman Expérimental,* seems to reveal an obtuseness to the disproof conveyed in his own novels which, in a French writer, is singular indeed. To be sure that author—whose powers in story-telling, rightly or wrongfully exercised, may be partly owing to the fact that he is not a critic—does in a measure concede something in the counsel that the novel should keep as close to reality *as it can*; a remark which may be interpreted with infinite latitude, and would, no doubt, have been cheerfully accepted by Dumas *père* or Mrs. Radcliffe. But to maintain in theory what he abandons in practice, to subscribe to rules and to work by instinct, is a proceeding not confined to the author of *Germinal* and *La Faute de l'Abbé Mouret.*

The reasons that make against such conformation of story-writing to scientific processes have been set forth so many times in examining the theories of the realist, that it is not necessary to recapitulate them here. Admitting the desirability, the impossibility of reproducing in its entirety the phantasmagoria of experience with infinite and atomic truth, without shadow, relevancy or subordination, is not the least of them. The fallacy appears to owe its origin to the just perception that with our widened knowledge of the universe and its forces, and man's position therein, narrative, to be artistically convincing, must adjust itself to the new alignment, as would also artistic works in form and colour, if further spectacles in their sphere could be presented. Nothing but the illusion of truth can permanently please, and when the old illusions begin to be penetrated, a more natural magic has to be supplied.

Creativeness in its full and ancient sense—the making of a thing or situation out of nothing that ever was before—is apparently ceasing to satisfy a world which no longer believes in the abnormal—ceasing at least to satisfy the van-couriers of taste; and creative fancy has accordingly to give more and more place to realism, that is to an artificiality distilled from the fruits of closest observation.

This is the meaning deducible from the work of the realists, however stringently they themselves may define realism in terms. Realism is an unfortunate, an ambiguous word, which has been taken up by literary society like a view-halloo, and has been assumed in some places to mean copyism, and in others pruriency, and has led to two classes of delineators being included in one condemnation.

Just as bad a word is one used to express a consequence of this development, namely 'brutality,' a term which, first applied by French critics, has since spread over the English school like the other. It aptly hits off the immediate expression of the thing meant; but it has the disadvantage of defining impartiality as a passion, and a plan as a caprice. It certainly is very far from truly expressing the aims and methods of conscientious and well-intentioned authors who, not-withstanding their excesses, errors, and rickety theories, attempt to narrate the *vérité vraié.*

To return for a moment to the theories of the scientific realists. Every friend to the novel should and must be in sympathy with their error, even while distinctly perceiving it. Though not true, it is well found. To advance realism as complete copyism, to call the idle trade of story-telling a science, is the hyperbolical flight of an admirable enthusiasm, the exaggerated cry of an honest reaction from the false, in which the truth has been impetuously approached and overleapt in fault of being lighted on.

Possibly, if we only wait, the third something, akin to perfection, will exhibit itself on its due pedestal. How that third something may be induced to hasten its presence, who shall say? Hardly the English critic.

But this appertains to the Art of novel-writing, and is outside the immediate subject. To return to the science. . . . Yet what is the use? Its very comprehensiveness renders the attempt to dwell upon it a futility. . . . An accomplished lady once confessed to the writer that she could never be in a room two minutes without knowing every article of furniture it contained and every detail in the attire of the inmates, and, when she left, remembering every remark. Here was a person, one might feel for the moment, who could prime herself to an unlimited extent, and at the briefest notice in the scientific data of fiction; one who, assuming her to have some slight artistic power, was a novelist. To explain why such a keen eye to the superficial does not imply a sensitiveness to the intrinsic, is a psychological matter beyond the scope of these notes; but that a blindness to material particulars often accompanies a quick perception of the more ethereal characteristics of humanity, experience continually shows.

A sight for the finer qualities of existence, an ear for the 'still sad music of humanity' are not to be acquired by the outer senses alone, close as their powers of photography may be. What cannot be discerned by eye and ear, what may be apprehended only by the mental tactility that comes from a sympathetic appreciation of life in all its manifestations, this is the gift which renders its possessor a more accurate delineator of human nature than many another with twice his powers and means of external observation, but without that sympathy. To see in half and quarter-views the whole picture, to catch from a few bars the whole tune, is the intuitive power that supplies the would-be story-teller with the scientific bases for his pursuit. He may not count the dishes at a feast or accurately estimate the value of the jewels in a lady's diadem; but through the smoke of those dishes, and the rays from those jewels, he sees written on the wall:

"We are such stuff
As dreams are made of, and our little life
Is rounded with a sleep."

Thus, as aforesaid, an attempt to set forth the Science of Fiction in calculable pages is a futility; it is to write a whole library of human philosophy, with instructions how to feel.

Once in a crowd a listener heard a needy and illiterate woman saying of another poor and haggard woman, who had lost her little son years before: 'You can see the ghost of that child in her face even now.'

That speaker was one who, though she could probably neither read nor write, had the true means towards the 'Science' of Fiction innate within her; a power of observation informed by a living heart. Had she been trained in the technicalities, she might have fashioned her view of morality with good effect: a reflection which leads to a conjecture that, perhaps, true novelists, like poets, are born, not made.

14

Galsworthy

John Galsworthy (1867-1933) came from an old Devonshire family, but he soon realised that "to think that birth, property, position—general superiority in sum—is anything but a piece of good luck is, of course, ridiculous." On their first meeting, Edward Garnett said to him, "Write about the English, for you've got it all inside you—all the keys that nobody turns in the locks." So he did. In his novels the group that make *The Forsyte Saga*—he gave us "the picture of the end of an epoch, the swan-song of the man of property." His plays, notably *The Silver Box, Strife, Justice, Loyalties, The Skin Game*, show his extraordinary mastery of stagecraft, an eager attempt to be scrupulously fair to both sides, and a desire to stimulate the public conscience. One who knew him summed him up as "the flower of the finest English traditions."

The extract given here is from a letter: a casual form preserving a pithy statement of important matter, the harvest of years of clear thinking and deep feeling.

Aug. 4th, 06.

. . . You ask me a poser about Morals and Art, so I'll answer you in platitudes.

They are both part of the machinery of life, both equally valuable and only in opposition in the following sense:

The artist takes life as he sees it, observes, connotes and stores with all his feelers, then out of his store constructs (creates) according to his temperament with the *primary* object of stirring the emotional nerves of his audience, and thereby directly, *actively giving pleasure.*

The moralist observes life, generalizes, notes what is wrong and forms laws, rules, and conventions, which by binding and checking the use or over use of the emotional nerves (*i.e.,* by negating individual pleasure) secondarily secures the pleasure of the greater number.

The process is in fact reversed.

The artist is active }
The moralist negative } as producers of pleasure.

Obviously, very few men are purely artists or purely moralists, perhaps none.

But all men are rather more one than the other. The antagonism only begins when personality comes into play, *i.e.*

A. (artist) is temperamentally opposed to M. (moralist) as a *man,* or they irritate each other, that's all, if they're both *extreme* types.

As to morals, what is moral to-day is immoral tomorrow, and that of course confuses things a bit. The artist there has the advantage in a manner of speaking because he is dealing with things that practically speaking do not change, *i.e.,* the laws of nature, and dealing with them with the senses, which also do not change (or so slowly that the changes do not count).

To take, for instance, the very useful Shakespeare. He is of course a supreme artist, but some people would call him also a great moralist. A moralist is essentially a man of an epoch of morals—it may not be his own epoch, it may be the next, but it is *an* epoch. Shakespeare, however, is dateless.

Most writers have a large dash of the moralist, all satirists have. But the two qualities in a writer are not necessarily in the least in opposition except as a matter of technique, that is of holding the balance firm and true so that both sides are done full justice to.

Does Garnett talk of an artist enjoying life? I think he must mean as a spectator endowed with great curiosity.

Conrad (a painter's writer) is perhaps the best specimen I can think of as a pure artist (there is practically nothing of the moralist in him) among moderns.

. . . Roughly speaking, the more a moralist is an artist, the longer he will live. As to the converse, well, those Artists so great that they are cosmic and deal in Nature's morals (not man's), such as Shakespeare and Homer, survive; but most surviving books and authors have been a blend of Artist and Moralist. Perhaps you have been inclined to use morals in the sense of *Nature's* morals; if so get out of the habit—it's a vague, bad use of the word—*mores*: customs, fashions. . . .

15
Eliot

T. S. Eliot (b. 1888), though born in America, came to live here in 1913, and became a British subject in 1927. He is now one of the most important living poets, and probably the one with the greatest influence on the poetry of To-day and To-morrow. His *Prufrock* poems of 1917 provided a complete break with nineteenth-century tradition: they gave the reader something new, something arresting, something intellectual, and something vital. *The Waste Land* of 1922 established him as the leading poet expressing the spirit of this age in a new way, the creation of this age. So pervasive is his example and precept that to many readers any new poem which betrays no realisation of the new fields and new voices created by Mr. Eliot seems an anachronism.

The Rock (1924) showed us that Mr. Eliot could succeed in another way, poetic drama, a no-man's-land where so many poets have abandoned unburied failures. *Murder in the Cathedral* astonished pessimists by proving that a play in verse could move audiences of ordinary theatre-goers. A serious man treated serious subjects—even dared to write with a mystical bias—and the ordinary man found it enjoyable and stimulating! His Aristophanic Melodrama, *Sweeney Agonistes,* showed he is not limited to one type of play.

We ought to be proud of Mr. Eliot as this age's greatest critic. The growth of modern critical journals of high standards—*The Criterion, Scrutiny*—is due directly in one, indirectly in the other, to him. *The Sacred Wood* (1920) spread his influence to a wider circle. His *Selected Essays* is a counterpart to Arnold's *Essays in Criticism, Poetry and the Uses of Criticism* (1933) is his latest work. All his criticism repays study and re-reading, more so probably than that of any other living writer. We learn to admire his wide range, his integrity, his sureness, his detail. He reassesses the past in terms of the present and in terms of the whole of the past. Tradition, to him, does not mean merely Milton—Dryden—Wordsworth—Tennyson.

"How many critics are there," asks Mr. Leavis, "who have made any difference to one—improved one's apparatus, one's equipment, one's efficiency as a reader?" He gives Mr. Eliot as one of the few in the whole of our history: he "has not only refined the conception and methods of criticism; he has put into currency decisive reorganising and reorientating ideas and valuations."

He speaks highly of the value of literature, warning us that "The people which ceases to care for its literary inheritance becomes barbaric; the people which ceases to produce literature ceases to move in thought and sensibility." The occasion of the chosen essay is the publication of '*Metaphysical Lyrics and Poems of the Seventeenth Century*: Donne to Butler. Selected and edited by H. J. C. Grierson, 1928.' The principal poets represented are John Donne (1573-1631), Thomas Carew (1594-1639), Andrew Marvell (1621-1678), George Herbert (1593-1633). The Editor defines Metaphysical poetry, in the full sense of the term, as that which "has been inspired by a philosophical conception of the universe and the rôle assigned to the human spirit in the great drama of existence. These poems were written because 'the latest scientific and philosophical notions' laid hold on the mind and imagination of a great poet, unified and illumined his comprehension of life, intensified and heightened his personal consciousness of joy and sorrow, of hope and fear, by broadening their significance, revealing to him the history of his own soul a brief abstract of the drama of human destiny. ... Its themes are the simplest experiences of the surface of life, sorrow and joy, love and battle, the peace of the country, the bustle and stir of towns, but equally the boldest conceptions, the profoundest intuitions, the subtlest and most complex classifications and 'discourse of reason,' if into these, too, the poet can 'carry sensation,' make of them passionate experiences communicable in vivid and moving imagery, in rich and varied harmonies." The Editor accepts the application of such a description of Dante and Lucretius to the work of Donne, his contemporaries and followers, because it stresses "the more intellectual, less verbal, character of their wit compared with the conceits of the Elizabethans; the finer psychology of which their conceits are often the expression; their learned imagery; the argumentative, subtle evolution of their lyrics; above all, the peculiar blend of passion and thought, feeling and ratiocination which is their greatest achievement."

You will not find Metaphysical poetry in "The Golden Treasury," thanks to Palgrave and Tennyson. The eighteenth century and the nineteenth century abused or ignored it. Now these experiments "to stir the emotions by first stimulating a reader's mind . . . are again understandable." Mr. Eliot's theory is that "Donne invented an idiom which less original men could learn to talk, and which they went on talking until they talked it out, and Dryden imposed a new way of speech on the next hundred years." In his essay on *The Metaphysical Poets,* he attempts to show that Romantics and post-Romantics have distorted our sense of tradition.

The Metaphysical Poets

By collecting these poems from the work of a generation more often named than read, and more often read than profitably studied, Professor Grierson has rendered a service of' some importance. Certainly the reader will meet with many poems already preserved in other anthologies, at the same time that he discovers poems such as those of Aurelian Townshend or Lord Herbert of Cherbury here included. But the function of such an anthology as this is neither that of Professor Saintsbury's admirable edition of Caroline poets nor that of the *Oxford Book of English Verse*. Mr. Grierson's book is in itself a piece of criticism; and we think that he was right in including so many poems of Donne, elsewhere (though not in many editions) accessible, as documents in the case of 'metaphysical poetry.'

The phase has long done duty as a term of abuse, or as the label of a quaint and pleasant taste. The question is to what extent the so-called metaphysical formed a school (in our own time we should say a 'movement'), and how far this so-called school or movement is a digression from the main current?

Not only is it extremely difficult to define metaphysical poetry, but difficult to decide what poets practise it and in which of their verses. The poetry of Donne (to whom Marvell and Bishop King are sometimes nearer than any of the other authors) is late Elizabethan, its feeling often very close to that of Chapman. The 'courtly' poetry is derivative from Johnson, who borrowed liberally from the Latin; it expires in the next century with the sentiment and witticism of prior. There is finally the devotional verse of Herbert, Vaughan, and Crashaw (echoed long after by Christina Rossetti and Francis Thompson): Crashaw, sometimes more profound and less sectarian than the others, has a quality which returns through the Elizabethan period to the early Italians. It is difficult to find any precise use of metaphor, simile or other conceit, which is common to all the poets and at the same time important enough as an element of style to isolate these poets as a group, Donne, and often Cowley, employ a device which is sometimes considered characteristically 'metaphysical'; the elaboration (contrasted with the condensation) of a figure of speech to the furthest stage to which ingenuity can carry it. Thus Cowley develops the commonplace comparison of the world to a chess-board through long stanzas *(To Destiny),* and Donne, with more grace, in *A Valediction,* the comparison of two lovers to a pair of compasses. But elsewhere we find, instead of the mere explication of the content of a comparison, a development by rapid association of thought which requires considerable agility on the part of the reader.

On a round ball

A u orkeman that hath copies by, can lay
An Europe, Afrique, and an Asia,
And quickly make that which was nothing, All,
So doth each teare,
Which thee doth weare,

A globe, yea world by that impression grow,
Till thy tears mixt with mine doe overflow
This world, by waters sent from thee, my heaven dissolved so.

Here we find at least two connexions which are not implicit in the first figure, but are forced upon it by the poet: from the geographer's globe to the tear, and from the tear to the deluge. On the other hand, some of Donne's most successful and characteristic efforts are secured by brief words and sudden contrasts:

A bracelet of bright hair about the bone,

where the most powerful effect is produced by the sudden contrasts of associations of 'bright hair' and of 'bone.' This telescoping of images and multiplied associations is characteristic of the phrase of some of the dramatists of the period which Donne knew: not to mention Shakespeare, it is frequent in Middleton; Webster, and Tourneur, and is one of the sources of the vitality of their language.

Johnson, who employed the term 'metaphysical poets,' apparently having Donne, Cleveland, and Cowley chiefly in mind, remarks of them that 'the most heterogeneous ideas are yoked by violence together.' The force of this impeachment lies in the failure of the conjunction, the fact that often the ideas are yoked but not united; and if we are to judge of styles of poetry by their abuse, enough examples may be found in Cleveland to justify Johnson's condemnation. But a degree of heterogeneity of material compelled into unity by the operation of the poet's mind is omnipresent in poetry. We need not select for illustration such a line as:

Notre âme est un fois trois-mâts cherchant son I carie;

we may find it in some of the best lines of Johnson himself (*The Vanity of Human Wishes*):

His fate was destined to a barren strand,
A petty fortress, and a dubious hand;
He left a name at which the world grew pale,
To point a moral, or adorn a tale.

where the effect is due to a contrast of ideas, different in degree but the same in principle, as that which Johnson mildly reprehended. And in one of the finest poems of the age (a poem which could not have been written in any other age), the *Exequy* of Bishop King, the extended comparison is used with perfect success: the idea and the simile become one, in the passage in which the Bishop illustrates his impatience to see his dead wife, under the figure of a journey:

Stay for me there; I will not faille
To meet thee in that hollow Vale.
And think not much of my delay;
I am already on the way,
And follow thee with all the speed
Desire can make, or sorrows breed.
Each minute is a short degree,
And ev'ry home a step towards thee.
At night when I betake to rest,
Next morn I rise nearer my West
Of life, almost by eight homes sail,
Than when sleep breath'd his drowsy gale . . . .
But heark! My Pulse, like a soft Drum
Beats my approach, tells Thee I come;
And slow howere my marches be,
I shall at last sit down by Thee.

(In the last few lines there is that effect of terror which is several times attained by one of Bishop King's admirers, Edgar Poe.) Again, we may justly take these quatrains from Lord Herbert's Ode, stanzas which would, we think, be immediately pronounced to be of the metaphysical school:

So when from hence we shall be gone,
  And be no more, nor you, nor I,
  As one another's mystery,
Each shall be both, yet both but one.

This said, in her up-lifted face,
  Her eyes, which did that beauty crown,

Were like two starrs, that having faln down
Look up again to find their place:

While such a moveless silent peace
Did seize on their becalméd sense,
One would have thought some influence
Their ravished spirits did possess.

There is nothing in these lines (with the possible exception of the stars, a simile not at once grasped, but lovely and justified) which fits Johnson's general observations on the metaphysical poets in his essay on Cowley. A good deal resides in the richness of association which is at the same time borrowed from and given to the word 'becalmed'; but the meaning is clear, the language simple and elegant. It is to be observed that the language of these poets is as a rule simple and pure; in the verse of George Herbert this simplicity is carried as far as it can go—a simplicity emulated without success by numerous modern poets. The *structure* of the sentences, on the other hand, is sometimes far from simple, but this is not a vice; it is a fidelity to thought and feeling. The effect, at its best, is far less artificial than that of an ode by Gray. And as this fidelity induces variety of thought and feeling, so it induces variety of music. We doubt whether, in the eighteenth century, could be found two poems in nominally the same metre, as dissimilar as Marvell's *Coy Mistress* and Crashaw's *Saint Teresa;* the one producing an effect of great speed by the use of short syllables, and the other an ecclesiastical solemnity by the use of long ones:

Love thou art absolute sole lord
Of life and death.

If so shrewd and sensitive (though so limited) a critic as Johnson failed to define metaphysical poetry by its faults, it is worthwhile to enquire whether we may not have more success by adopting the opposite method: by assuming that the poets of the seventeenth century (up to the Revolution) were the direct and normal development of the precedent age; and, without prejudicing their case by the term 'meta-physical,' consider whether their virtue was not something permanently valuable, which subsequently disappeared, but ought not to have disappeared. Johnson has hit, perhaps by accident, on one of their peculiarities, when he observes that 'their attempts were always analytic'; he would not agree that, after the dissociation, they put the material together again in a new unity.

It is certain that the dramatic verse of the later Elizabethan and early Jacobean poets expresses a degree of development of sensibility which is not found in any of the prose, good as it often is. If we except Marlowe, a man of prodigious intelligence, these dramatists were directly or indirectly (it is at least a tenable theory) affected by Montaigne. Even if we except also Johnson and Chapman, these two were notably erudite, and were notably men who incorporated their erudition into their sensibility: their mode of feeling was directly and freshly altered by their reading and thought. In Chapman especially there is a direct sensuous apprehension of thought, or a re-creation of thought into feeling, which is exactly what we find in Donne:

in this one thing, all the discipline
Of manners and of manhood is contained;
A man to join himself with th' Universe
In his main sway, and make in all things fit
One with that All, and go on, round as it;
Not plucking from the whole his wretched part,
And into straits, or into naught revert,
Wishing the complete universe might be
Subject to such a rag of it as he;
But to consider great necessity.

We compare this with some modern passage:

No, when the fight begins within himself,
A man's worth something. God stoops o'er his head,
Satan looks up between his feet—both tug—
He's left, himself, i' the middle; the soul wakes
And grows. Prolong that battle through his life.

It is perhaps somewhat less fair, though very tempting (as both poets are concerned with the perpetuation of love by offspring), to compare with the stanzas already quoted from Lord Herbert's Ode the following from Tennyson:

One walked between his wife and child,
With measured footfall firm and mild,
And now and then he gravely smiled.
The prudent partner of his blood
Leaned on him, faithful, gentle, good,
Wearing the rose of womanhood.
And in their double love secure,
The little maiden walked demure,
Pacing with downward eyelids pure.
These three made unity so sweet,
My frozen heart began to beat,
Remembering its ancient heat.

The difference is not a simple difference of degree between poets. It is something which had happened to the mind of England between the time of Donne or Lord Herbert of Cherbury and the time of Tennyson and Browning; it is the difference between the intellectual poet and the reflective poet. Tennyson and Browning are poets, they think; but they do not feel their thought as immediately as the odour of a rose. A thought to Donne was an experience; it modified his sensibility. When a poet's mind is perfectly equipped for its work, it is constantly amalgamating disparate experience; the ordinary man's experience is chaotic, irregular, and fragmentary. The latter falls in love, or reads Spinoza, and these two experiences have nothing to do with each other, or with the noise of the typewriter or the smell of cooking; in the mind of the poet these experiences are always forming new wholes.

We may express the difference by the following theory: the poets of the seventeenth century, the successors of the dramatists of the sixteenth, possessed a mechanism of sensibility which could devour any kind of experience. They are simple, artificial, difficult, or fantastic, as their predecessors were; no less nor more than Dante, Guido Cavalcanti, Guinicelli, or Cino. In the seventeenth century a dissociation of sensibility set in, from which we have never recovered; and this dissociation, as is natural, was aggravated by the influence of the two most powerful poets of the century, Milton and Dryden. Each of these men performed certain poetic functions so magnificently well that the magnitude of the effect concealed the absence of others. The language went on and in some respects improved: the best verse of Collins, Gray, Johnson, and even Goldsmith satisfies some of our fastidious demands better than that of Donne or Marvell or King. But while the language became more refined, the feeling became more crude. The feeling, the sensibility, expressed in the *Country Churchyard* (to say nothing of Tennyson and Browning) is cruder than that in the *Coy Mistress*.

The second effect of the influence of Milton and Dryden followed from the first, and was therefore slow in manifestation. The sentimental age began early in the eighteenth century, and continued. The poets revolted against the ratiocinative, the descriptive; they thought and felt by fits, unbalanced; they reflected. In one or two passages of Shelley's *Triumph of Life*, in the second *Hyperion*, there are traces of a struggle toward unification of sensibility. But Keats and Shelley died, and Tennyson and Browning ruminated.

After this brief exposition of a theory—too brief, perhaps, to carry conviction—we may ask, what would have been the fate of the 'metaphysical' had the current of poetry descended in a direct line from them, as it descended in a direct line to them? They would not, certainly, be classified as metaphysical. The possible interests of a poet are unlimited; the more intelligent he is the better; the more intelligent he is the more likely that he will have interests: our only condition is that he turn them into poetry, and not merely meditate on them poetically. A philosophical theory which has entered into poetry is established, for its truth or falsity in one sense ceases to matter, and its truth in another sense is proved. The poets in question have, like other poets, various faults. But they were, at best, engaged in the task of trying to find the verbal equivalent for states of mind and feeling. And this means both that they are more mature, and that they wear better, than later poets of certainly not less literary ability.

It is not a permanent necessity that poets should be interested in philosophy, or in any other subject. We can only say that it appears likely that poets in our civilization, as it exists at present, must be *difficult.* Our civilization comprehends great variety and complexity, and this variety and complexity, playing upon a refined sensibility, must produce various and complex results. The poet must become more and more comprehensive, more allusive, more indirect, in order to force, to dislocate if necessary, language into his meaning. (A brilliant and extreme statement of this view, with which it is not requisite to associate oneself, is that of M. Jean Epstein, *La Poèsie d'aujourd'hui.)* Hence, we get something which looks very much like the conceit—we get, in fact, a method curiously similar to that of the 'metaphysical poets,' similar also in its use of obscure words and of simple phrasing:

O géraniums diaphanes, guerroyeurs sortilèges,
Sacrilèges monomanes!
Emballages, dévergondages, douches! 0 pressoirs
Des vendanges des grands soirs!
Layettes aux abois,
Thyrses au fond des bois!
Transfusions, représailles,
Relevailles, compresses et l'éternal potion,
Angèlus! n'en pouvoir plus
De débâcles nuptiales! de débâcles nuptiales!

The same poet could also write simply:

Elle est bien loin, elle pleure,
Le grand vent se lament aussi. . . .

Jules Laforgue, and Tristram Corbiére in many of his poems, are nearer to the 'school of Donne' than any modern English poet. But poets more classical than they have the same essential quality of transmuting ideas into sensations, of transforming an observation into a state of mind.

Pour l'enfant, amoureux de cartes et d'estampes,
L'univers est ègal à son vaste appetit.
Ah, que le monde est grand à la clarté des lampes!
Aux yeux du souvenir que le mond est petit!

In French literature the great master of the seventeenth century—Racine—and the great master of the nineteenth—Baudelaire—are in some ways more like each other than they are like anyone else. The greatest two masters of diction are also the greatest two psychologists, the most curious explorers of the soul. It is interesting to speculate whether it is not a misfortune that two of the greatest masters of diction in our own language, Milton and Dryden, triumph with a dazzling disregard of the soul. If we continued to produce Miltons and Drydens it might not so much matter, but as things are it is a pity that English poetry has remained so incomplete. Those who object to the 'artificiality' of Milton or Dryden sometimes tell us to 'look into our hearts and write.' But that is not looking deep enough; Racine or Donne looked into a good deal more than the heart. One must look into the cerebral cortex, the nervous system, and the digestive tracts.

May we not conclude, then, that Donne, Crashaw, Vaughan, Herbert and Lord Herbert, Marvell, King, Cowley at his best, are in the direct current of English poetry, and that their faults should be reprimanded by this standard rather than coddled by antiquarian affection? They have been enough praised in terms which are implicit limitations because they are 'meta-physical' or 'witty,' 'quaint' or 'obscure,' though at their best they have not these attributes more than other serious poets. On the other hand, we must not reject the criticism of Johnson (a dangerous person to disagree with) without having mastered it, without having assimilated the Johnsonian canons of taste. In reading the celebrated passage in his essay on Cowley we must remember that by wit he clearly means something more serious than we usually mean to-day; in his criticism of their versification we must remember in what a narrow discipline he was trained, but also how well-trained; we must remember that Johnson tortures chiefly the chief offenders, Cowley and Cleveland. It would be a fruitful work, and one requiring a substantial book, to break up the classification of Johnson (for there has been none since) and exhibit these poems in all their difference of kind and of degree, from the massive music of Donne to the faint, pleasing tinkle of Aurelian Townshend—whose *Dialogue between a Pilgrim and Time* is one of the few regrettable omissions from the excellent anthology of Professor Grierson.

The following is added

for purposes of comparison.

Dr. Johnson, on the Metaphysical Poets, in the section devoted to Cowley in *Lives of the English Poets.*

The metaphysical poets were men of learning, and to show their learning was their whole endeavour; but, unluckily resolving to show it in rhyme, instead of writing poetry they only wrote verses, and very often such verses as stood the trial of the finger better than of the ear; for the modulation was so imperfect, that they were only found to be verses by counting the syllables.

[Johnson objects to Pope's definition of wit as "that which has been often thought, but was never before so well-expressed" because wit is thus reduced "from strength of thought to happiness of language."]

If by a more noble and more adequate conception, that be considered as wit which is at once natural and new, that which, though not obvious, is, upon its first production, acknowledged to be just; if it be that which he that never found it, wonders how he missed; to wit of this kind the metaphysical poets have seldom risen. Their thoughts are often new, but seldom natural; they are not obvious, but neither are they just; and the reader, far from wondering that he missed them, wonders more frequently by what perverseness of industry they were ever found.

But wit . . . may be . . . considered as a kind of *discordia concors*; a combination of dissimilar images, or discovery of occult resemblances in things apparently unlike. Of wit, thus defined, they have more than enough. The most heterogeneous ideas are yoked by violence together; nature and art are ransacked for illustrations, comparisons and allusions; their learning instructs, and their subtlety surprises; but the reader commonly thinks his improvement dearly bought, and, though he sometimes admires, is seldom pleased. . . . Their wish was only to say what they hoped had never been said before.

. . . Yet great labour, directed by great abilities, is never wholly lost: if they frequently threw away their wit upon false conceits, they likewise sometimes struck out unexpected truth: if their conceits were farfetched, they were often worth the carriage. To write on their plan, it was at least necessary to read and think. No man could be a metaphysical poet, nor assume the dignity of a writer, by descriptions copied from descriptions, by imitations borrowed from imitations, by traditional imagery and hereditary similes, by readiness of rhyme and volubility of syllables.

. . . They were in very little care to clothe their notions with elegance of dress, and therefore miss the notice and praise which are often gained by those, who think less, but are more diligent to adorn their thoughts.

16

Read

Herbert Read (b. 1893) has served the Arts so long and so well that many admire and follow him, and his adversaries respect him. He is a man of many activities: a professor, an expert on pottery, a defender of modern art, an editor of valuable books such as *Art and Society,* an interpreter of Wordsworth, part-editor of *The London Book of English Prose* (the best of its kind), a poet well represented in intelligent, up-to-date anthologies, and a critic in general, as in *In Defence of Shelley, and Other Essays,* from which this extract—the third section of a study of G. M. Hopkins—is taken. He avoids merely raising old dust on well-trodden paths, but leads us persuasively over newer ground, making the way seem clear.

Gerard Manley Hopkins (1844-1889) might have been a musician or a painter: he became a priest in 1877, and remained a poet, a man of character, intelligence, and originality to the end. He kept in touch with his friends, Canon R. W. Dixon, Dr. Robert Bridges, and Coventry Patmore: his correspondence with the second of the three both enables us to learn of his charm and depth and gives many reasoned conclusions on topics of literary criticism from a highly individual mind.

His poems remained in manuscript for many years, Dr. Bridges having the power to decide when and how to launch them in a world for which, at the time of the poet's death, they were apparently too advanced, too strange. After very cautiously introducing them into his anthologies, Bridges edited and published a volume of Hopkins's poems in 1918. Slowly—extremely so—they made their way. "Poets and critics began to occupy themselves more strenuously with Hopkins's work. He was called, and actually was, an influence. He was discussed and actually read. He was written about and actually remembered." Thus arises the paradox that one of the great influences in modern poetry is the work of a man, who died in 1889, that one who has been called the greatest of the Victorians really first came to life in this century.

The casual reader experiences a shock in meeting the poems of Hopkins for the first time. Professor Read's orderly exposition is an example of the critic's work in helping lame dogs over stiles.

The Poetry of Gerard Manley Hopkins

The terrible sincerity of the process of Hopkins's thought invariably led him to an originality of expression which rejected the ready-made counters of contemporary poetics. His originality in this respect is both verbal and metrical, and perhaps the innovations he introduced into metre prevent more than anything else the appreciation of his poetry. Except for a few early poems, which need not be taken into account, practically every poem written by Hopkins presents rhythmical irregularities. The poet himself attempted a theoretical justification of these, and it is an extremely ingenious piece of work. But there can be no possible doubt—and it is most important to emphasize this—that the rhythm of Hopkins's poems, considered individually, was intuitive in origin:

> Since all the maker of man
> Is law's indifference.

The theory was invented later to justify his actual powers. The preface in which he advances his theories was written about 1883—in the midst, that is to say, of his main creative period. He begins by saying that his poems are written some in Running Rhythm, by which he means the common rhythm in English use, and some in Sprung Rhythm, and some in a mixture of the two. He proceeds to define what he means by these terms, and I will do the same, using as far as possible his own words and taking his own poems as illustrations.

Common English rhythm, the standard rhythm in use from the sixteenth to the nineteenth centuries, is measured by feet of either two or three syllables and never more or less. Every foot has one principal stress or accent, and for purposes of scanning Hopkins held that it is a great convenience to follow the example of music and take the stress always first, as the accent or chief accent always comes first in a musical bar. If this is done there will be in common English verse only two possible feet—the so-called Trochaic and Dactylic, though these two may sometimes be mixed.

> But because [Hopkins goes on to explain] verse written strictly in these feet and by these principles will become same and tame, the poets have brought in licences and departures from rule to give variety. . . . These irregularities are chiefly Reversed or Counterpoint Rhythm, which two things are two steps or degrees of licence in the same kind.

By a reversed foot, he goes on to explain, perhaps unnecessarily,

> I mean putting the stress where, to judge from the rest of the measure, the slack should be, and the slack where the stress; and this is done freely at the beginning of the line, and, in the course of a line, after the pause; only scarcely ever in the second foot and never in the last, for these places are characteristic and sensitive and cannot well be touched.

The following two verses from *The Habit of Perfection,* one of Hopkins's early poems, show an isolated instance of a reversed foot in the third line; otherwise it is in standard trochaic metre:

> Elected Silence, sing to me,
> And beat upon my whorlèd ear,
> Pipe me to pastures still and be
> The music that I care to hear.

Shape nothing, lips; be lovely-dumb;
It is the shut, the curfew sent
From there where all surrenders come
Which only makes you eloquent?

This is, of course, all very simple and unremarkable, and has been the practice of every good poet from Chaucer down: as Hopkins says, it is nothing but the irregularity which all growth and motion shows.

If, however, the reversal is repeated in two feet running, especially so as to include the sensitive second foot, it must be due either to great want of ear or else it is a calculated effect, the super-inducing or *mounting* of a new rhythm upon the old; and since the new or mounted rhythm is actually heard, and at the same time the mind naturally supplies 'the standard rhythm which by rights we should be hearing,' two rhythms are in some manner running at once and we have something answerable to counterpoint in music, which is two or more strains of tune going on together, and this is Counterpoint Rhythm. Of this kind of verse Milton is the great master, and the choruses of *Samson Agonistes* are written throughout in it. . . .

Let us take a simple example from Hopkins: *God's Grandeur:*

The world is charged with the grandeur of God.
It will flame out, like shining from shook foil;
It gathers to a greatness, like the ooze of oil Crushed.
Why do men then now not rack his rod? Generations have trod, have trod, have trod;
And all is smeared with trade; bleared, smeared with toil;
And wears man's smudge and shares man's smell: the soil
Is bare now, nor can foot feel, being shod.

And for all this, nature is never spent;
There lives the dearest freshness deep down things;
And though the last lights off the black West went,
Oh, morning, at the brown brink eastward, springs—
Because the Holy Ghost over the bent

World broods with warm breast and with, ah! bright wings.

Here again the underlying measure is standard iambic; but in nearly every line of the Sonnet, a foot is reversed and we hear against the running rhythm, this rhythm pointed counter to the proper flow.

If you counterpoint throughout a poem, the original rhythm will be destroyed or lost, and that is actually what happens in the choruses of *Samson Agonistes*. Then the result is probably what Hopkins calls Sprung Rhythm.

By this he meant rhythm measured by feet of from one to four syllables. In exceptional cases, for particular effects, you may have feet of any number of weak or slack syllables. The stress in each foot falls on the first syllable—or on the only syllable if there is only one. The result is a rhythm of incomparable freedom: any two stresses may either follow one another running or may be divided by one, two, or three slack syllables. The feet are assumed to be equally long or strong, and their seeming inequality is made up by pause or stressing. Such rhythm cannot be counterpointed. Note also that it is natural for the lines to be *rove over* as Hopkins expressed it, that is, for the scanning of each line immediately to take up that of the one before, so that if the first has one or more syllables at its end, the second must have so many less at its beginning; and in fact the scanning runs on without break from the beginning of a stanza to the end, and all the stanza is one long strain, though written in lines asunder.

Further, Hopkins claims that two licences are natural to Sprung Rhythm. The one is rests, as in music, the other is *hangers* or *outrides,* that is one, two, or three slack syllables added to a foot and not counted in the normal scanning. They are so-called because they seem to hang below the line or ride forward or backward from it in another dimension than the line itself.

Felix Randal is a typical example of such rhythm:

Felix Randal, the furrier, O he is dead then? my duty all ended,

Who have watched his mould of man, big-boned and hardy-handsome,

Pining, pining, till time when reason rambled in it and some

Fatal four disorders, fleshed there, all contended?
Sickness broke him. Impatient he cursed at first, but mended,
Being anointed and all; though a heavenlier heart began some
Months earlier, since I had our sweet reprieve and ransom
Tendered to him. Ah well, God rest him all road ever he offended!

This seeing the sick endears them to us, us too it endears,
My tongue had taught thee comfort, touch had quenched thy tears,
Thy tears had touched my heart, child, Felix, poor Felix Randal;

How far from them forethought of, all thy more boisterous years,
When thou at the random grim forge, powerful amidst peers,
Didst fettle for the great grey dray horse his bright and battering sandal!

Hopkins himself observed about such rhythm that it is the most natural of things. It is the rhythm of common speech and of written prose, when rhythm is perceived in them. It is the rhythm of all but the most monotonously regular music, so that it arises in the words of choruses and refrains and in songs written closely to music. It is found in nursery rhymes, weather saws, and so on . . . and it arises in common verse when reversed or counterpointed. And, I would add, it is the rhythm of all the genuine *vers libre* or free verse which has arisen since Hopkins's time.

This being so, the question arises: how came such a natural and universal rhythm to be neglected in English poetry? Perhaps we should rather ask: how did the standard Running Rhythm come into existence? and having once come into existence, why did it become such a fixed norm? Not only Greek and Latin lyric verse, which are in Sprung Rhythm, but the whole tradition of Teutonic and Norse poetry favours the principle of sprung rhythm. So that we may say that the tradition of sprung rhythm to which Hopkins returned has a tradition within our own linguistic world at least twice as long as the tradition of running rhythm. For running rhythm was only established in England in the sixteenth century, whereas sprung rhythm had existed for at least eight centuries before that time. Our early metre is usually known as alliterative, and is entirely without rhyme. In this metre each line is divided by a pause, and each half line contains two or more stresses, and an irregular number of slacks: the stresses in each whole line have the same initial sounds, and on account of this the metre is called alliterative. The only difference between this metre and Hopkins is that Hopkins adds rhyme, and uses alliteration on no fixed principle. But it will already have been noticed that he nevertheless makes considerable use of alliteration. In a few of his poems the total effect of alliteration is not much less than in a purely alliterative poem like *Piers Plowman*. *The Windhover* is a supreme example:

I caught this morning morning's minion, kingdom
of daylight's dauphin, dapple-dawn-drawn Falcon, in his riding
of the rolling level underneath him steady air, and striding
High there, how he rung upon the rein of a wimpling wing
In his ecstasy! Then off, off forth on swing,
As a skate's heel sweeps smooth on a bow-bend: the hurl and gliding
Rebuffed the big wind. My heart in hiding
Stirred for a bird,—the achieve of, the mastery of the thing!
Brute beauty and valour and act, oh, air, pride, plume, here
Buckle! *And* the fire that breaks from thee then, a billion
Times more lovelier, more dangerous, O my chevalier!
No wonder of it: sheer plod makes plough down sillion
Shine, and blue-break embers, ah my dear,
Fall, gall themselves, and gash gold-vermilion.

In short we might say that Hopkins is eager to use every device the language can hold to increase the force of his rhythm and the richness of his phrasing. Point, counterpoint, rests, running-over rhythms, hangers or outrides, slurs; end-rhymes, internal rhymes, assonance and alliteration—all are used to make the verse sparkle like rich irregular crystals in the gleaming flow of the poet's limpid thought.

The other aspect of his technique is one which, to my way of thinking, is still more central to the poetic reality: I mean his fresh and individual vocabulary. No true poet hesitates to invent words when his sensibility finds no satisfaction in current phrases. Words like 'shivelight' and 'firedint' are probably such inventions. But most of Hopkins's innovations are in the nature of new combinations of existing words, sometimes contracted similes, or metaphors, and in this respect his vocabulary has a surface similarity to that of James Joyce. Examples of such phrases are to be found in almost every poem: 'the bead-bonny ash', 'fallow-bootfellow,' 'windlaced,' 'churlsgrace,' 'foot-fretted,' 'clammyish lashtender combe,' 'wildworth,' and so on. Commoner phrases like 'beetle-browed' or 'star-eyed' are of the same kind, made in the same way, and freely used by him. Here again an explanation would take us far beyond the immediate subject; for it concerns the original nature of poetry itself— the emotional sound-complex uttered in primitive self-expression. Mr. Williams, whose graceful and appreciative introduction to the second edition of the poems is a fair corrective to the pedantic undertones of Dr. Bridges in the first edition, has an excellent description of the phenomenon as it appeared in the composition of Hopkins's verse. 'It is as if the imagination, seeking for expression, had found both verb and substantive at one rush, had begun almost to say them at once, and had separated them only because the intellect had reduced the original unity into divided but related sounds.' Poetry can only be renewed by discovering the original sense of word-formation: the words do not come pat in great poetry, but are torn out of the context of experience; they are not in the poet's mind but in the nature of the things he describes. 'You must know,' said Hopkins himself, 'that words like *charm* and *enchantment* will not do: the thought is of beauty as of something that can be physically kept and lost, and by physical things only, like keys; then the things must come from the *mundus muliebris*; and thirdly they must not be markedly old-fashioned. You will see that this limits the choice of words very much indeed.'

Of Hopkins's imagery, there is not much in general to be said, but that 'not much' is all. He had that acute and sharp sensuous awareness essential to all great poets. He was physically aware of textures, surfaces, colours, and patterns of every kind; aware acutely of earth's diurnal course, of growth and decay, of animality in man and of vitality in all things. Everywhere there is passionate apprehension, passionate expression, and equally that passion for form without which these other passions are spendthrift. But the form is inherent in the passion. 'For,' as Emerson remarked with his occasional deep insight, 'it is not metres, but a metre-making argument, that makes a poem—a thought so passionate and alive, that, like the spirit of a plant or an animal, it has an architecture of its own, and adorns nature with a new thing.'

17
Auden

W. H. Auden (b. 1907) is a very active figure, who has made his presence felt through such works as *The Orators* and *The Poet's Tongue* (in collaboration)—that striking attempt to break away from "The Golden Treasury" and all that it implies. The sincerity, individuality, and forcefulness of his poetry make a deep impression: his poem "Spain" deservedly won the King's Medal for the most outstanding book of poetry published in 1936. With Christopher Isherwood as collaborator, he has written verse plays that stimulate both reader and theatre-goer—*The Dance of Death, The Ascent of F6*, and *The Dog Beneath the Skin*. His share in *Letters from Iceland* contributes largely to that book's charm. "The vitality of his talent, and its extraordinary suppleness and variety, make him one of the few young writers worth watching."

The extract chosen is part of his introduction to *Selected Poems of Robert Frost* (1936). Mr. Frost is an American poet, a friend of Edward Thomas, whose work strikes a new note and call for a revaluation of our ideas of "nature poetry." Mr. Auden's criticism is an example of a trend of modern thought—the reference of works of art to the social conditions of the time.

Nature Poetry

The term 'Nature Poetry' could not have been used as a critical label before the development of an industrial economy, that is to say, before the social life of the town and that of the country had become so specialized and so divergent in their interests as to seem separate fields of existence.

Before such a point is reached, there may be other divisions—there may be poetry by the learned, and popular poetry, the court poet and the ballad vendor— but not between the town and the country. There is no lack of reference in Homer or Dante or Shakespeare to natural objects and natural scenery, but these are not introduced as something special, but as a proper background to normal human activities. Man is naturally anthropocentric and interested in his kind and in things and animals only in so far as they contribute to his life and sustain him; he does not interest himself in things to the exclusion of people till his relations with the latter have become difficult or have broken down.

Nature poetry is a sign of social specialization and social strain:

> The world is too much with us, late and soon
> Getting and spending we lay waste our powers.

> If men were as much men as lizards are lizards
> They'd be worth looking at.

Corresponding to these two tendencies are two kinds of nature poets, the man who lives in the country because he has to, because he works there; and the sensitive, who lives in the country because he can afford to and because he dislikes the city. Wordsworth and Lawrence belong to the latter. The former can be again sub-divided into two classes, the landed gentleman who is responsible for his land but does not work it with his own hands, such as the Virgil of the Georgics, and the small farmer who works it himself. Of this last Robert Frost is almost the only representative. His qualities of irony and understatement, his mistrust of fine writing, are those of the practical man:

> For them there was really nothing sad.
> But though they rejoiced in the nest they kept,
> One had to be versed in country things
> Not to believe the phœbes wept.

His poems on natural objects, such as 'Birches,' 'Mending Wall,' or 'The Grindstone,' are always concerned with them not as foci for mystical mediation or starting-points for fantasy, but as things with which land on which man acts in the course of the daily work of gaining a livelihood. Hence also the slow pace of his verse, so unlike the energetic and violent insight of Lawrence. Nor is he, like Wordsworth, a poet who has had a vision in youth which he can spend the rest of his life in interpreting. His material is not given him in a rush at the beginning. What de la Mare wrote of Frost's friend, and to some extent pupil, Edward Thomas, applies equally to him. "These poets tell us, not so much of rare exalted chosen moments, of fleeting inexplicable intuitions, but of his daily and, one might say, common experience." There is very little poetry about the country which one can feel confident would be immediately understood and appreciated by countrymen, but of these poems one is certain. They are not written for townees.

Appendix

ARISTOTLE AND THE UNITIES

To Aristotle (d. 322 B.C.) is attributed *The Poetics,* written not later than 330 B.C., after Aeschylus, Sophocles, and Euripides had fixed the form and nature of Tragedy, but before Menander had introduced a new style of Comedy. It could not, then, be "the last word" even on Greek drama. *The Poetics* is a fragment, and not necessarily the work of Aristotle. Many think it represents lecture notes.

Although the work seems to be an answer to Plato's challenge to show that poetry is "helpful to society and the life of man," it is always restrained and cool. It expresses the mind of a clear thinker, keen to find the essence of the classes he loves to establish: but he was dealing with literature that did fall with ease into clear-cut divisions.

Much of what is in *The Poetics* is true of all time. In the past the author has been overvalued: to-day he is too readily dismissed as one of merely academic interest. Many critical "ideas" have been unjustly fathered on him, particularly those dealing with *The Three Unities.* In *The Poetics* we read that it was the practice to limit the duration of the action in a Tragedy to one revolution of the sun. That is the basis of 'The Unity of Time': those of Place and Action are really due to commentators such as Castelvetro (1570). That the theories should be elevated into laws is not Aristotle's fault.

Ben Jonson knew too much to ascribe the Unities to Aristotle, and knew that the exuberant age of Elizabeth needed the restraint they imposed. "Other things being equal," said Mr. Ashley Dukes, in 1926, "it is always better to minimize the changes of scene and to reduce as far as possible the intervals that are supposed to elapse outside the visible movement."

In the seventeenth century French authors and critics, having read of the Unities in Roman writings, tried to find support for them in *The Poetics.* After a time of lawlessness in the theatre, everyone was ready for some healthy restraint, just as in the nineteenth century there was a feeling for liberty after long bondage. In a period of deportment, a leading writer like Corneille felt he had to bow to public opinion—to Richelieu and the Academy. He accepted the learner's rules: his success almost sanctified these rules.

By Dryden's day, many in England were ready to follow French precept and practice. Dryden takes an independent attitude. He allows Crites to state the case for the Unities in its extreme form. The Unity of Time, Crites claims, limits the time of the action of the play to twenty-four hours: therefore the post must see "that no act should be imagined to exceed the time in which it is represented on the stage; and that the intervals and irregularities of time be supposed to fall out between the acts." He commends the practice of setting the audience "at the post where the race is to be concluded."

After allowing that "painted scenes" may cheat the fancy, and saying of the Unity of Place that "the ancients meant by it that the scene ought to be continued through the play, in the same place where it was laid down in the beginning," he praises the French because the scene is never changed in the course of an act—"if the act begins in a garden, a street, or a chamber, 'tis ended in the same place."

As for the Unity of Action—"The poet is to aim at one great and complete action." Two actions would make two plays and prevent unity. He approves of many actions subservient to the great one — "underplots." Lisideius, in the same Essay, reminds us that "every alteration or crossing of a design, every new-sprung passion, and turn of it, is a part of the action, and much the noblest, except we conceive nothing to be action till the players come to blows."

Neander speaks for Dryden. He points out that Corneille complained "how much we are limited and constrained by 'the rules,' and how many beauties of the stage" are banished by them. Dryden charges French drama with dearth of plot and narrowness of imagination. "How many beautiful accidents might naturally happen in two or three days, which cannot arrive with any probability in the compass of twenty-four hours?" "Great and prudent persons" need time for the maturity of their designs. "If the scenes were interrupted, and the stage cleared for others to enter," French playwrights might introduce many beauties. He laughs at the absurdities caused by observance of the unities—such as bringing into the king's bed-chamber the meanest man in the kingdom, because the scene cannot be changed.

Dryden dares to challenge the theory that Tragedy must have "incidents arousing pity and fear"; he doubts "whether pity and terror are either the prime, or at least the only ends of Tragedy. 'Tis not enough that Aristotle had said so; for Aristotle drew his models from Sophocles and Euripides, and if he had seen ours might have changed his mind. For all the passions in their turn are to be set in a ferment." There spoke one who would not bow the knee. He ventures to suggest that the ancients, by "leaving love untouched," had given modern writers an opportunity of extending and improving drama.

Yet, long after Dryden's Essay, we find Dr. Johnson having to fight the same battles. "The truth is, that the spectators are always in their senses, and know, from the first act to the last, that the stage is only a stage, and that the players are only players. . . . Where is the absurdity of allowing that space to represent first Athens, and then Sicily, which was always known to be neither Sicily nor Athens, but a modern theatre?" Similarly—"A lapse of years is as easily conceived as a lapse of hours." He declines to weep because Shakespeare either did not know or did not observe the unities. "The unities of time and place are not essential to a just drama; . . . though they may sometimes conduce to pleasure, they are always to be sacrificed to the nobler beauties of variety and instruction." So we are left with the Unity of Action—for so long third in the race. A play with only one 'set' may appeal more to stage managers than one requiring many—but that is another story. The printed programme can smooth over intervals of months and years, and do the work of many of those work a day lines at the beginning of an act in an old play. And as for regarding rules of any kind as laws—hear D. H. Lawrence:—

"Tell Arnold Bennett that all rules of construction hold good only for novels which are copies of other novels. A book which is not a copy of others' books has its own construction, and what he calls faults, he being an old imitator, I call characteristics."

Questions

I

1. Aristotle defined Tragedy as the representation of "an action that is serious and . . . complete in itself; in language with pleasurable accessories . . . ; in a dramatic, not in a narrative form . . ." making a "complete whole, with its several incidents so closely connected that the transpolar or withdrawal of any one of them will disjoin and dislocate the whole," choosing as its main figure "a man not pre-eminently virtuous and just, whose misfortune, however, is brought upon him not by vice and depravity but by some error of judgment."
   (*a*) Which of these features have been ignored in the Monk's definition?
   (*b*) To what extent is this accounted for by the fact that the *acting* of a whole tragedy was unknown at the time?
2. The Monk tells his seventeen tragedies in less time than is taken by one tale of other pilgrims. What thought could he has given to the art of story-telling or to the affect of the tragedies on the audience?
3. In view of the pilgrims' strong preference for something light and cheerful, account for the popularity of the following: (*a*) crime stories in newspapers and magazines; (*b*) the Chamber of Horrors at a waxwork show; (*c*) heavy, gloomy tunes, *e.g.*, 'Abide with me'; (*d*) having 'a good cry' in a cinema.
4. Would the pilgrims enjoy true stories of to-day such as that of the rise from humble origin of Lord Nuffield?
5. "Aston Villa's Tragic Slip"—newspaper headlines. What is implied by ' Tragic ' and by 'Tragedy' in the loose usage of the papers or of the man-in-the-street?
6. Are we to consider the Knight and the Host as critics, or as people who know what they like?

II

1. Which of Sidney's claims for Poetry do you consider (*a*) strongest, (*b*) weakest? Why?
2. What is the total effect of these claims?
3. Find in this extract evidence to show that—
   (*a*) Sidney regarded a play as something to be seen and heard.
   (*b*) He based his criticism on classical models, yet hoped that in time his own country would furnish plays that would serve as models.
   (*c*) He believed he was doing a disservice to the cause of Art by over-praising.
   (*d*) He was writing to an educated audience, appealing to the judicious.
   (*e*) He declined to talk in the air, but furnished illustrations wherever possible.
   (*f*) He was over-concerned that works of art should fall readily into prearranged pigeon-holes of Classification.
4. What would Sidney have said if he could have read these passages?
   (*a*) If you consider the historical plays of Shakespeare, they are rather so many chronicles of kings, or the business many times of thirty or forty years, cramped into a representation of two hours and an half; which is not to imitate or paint nature, but rather to draw her in miniature . . . ; this, instead of making a play delightful, renders it ridiculous. [Dryden, *Essay of Dramatic Poetry,* 1668.]
   (*b*) Not that I commend narrations in general,—but there are two sorts of them. One, of those things which are antecedent to the play, and are related to make the conduct of it more clear to us. But 'tis a fault to choose such subjects for the stage as will force us on that rock, because we see they are seldom listened to by the audience, and that is many times the ruin of the play;

for, being once let pass without attention, the audience can never recover themselves to understand the plot: and indeed it is somewhat unreasonable that they should be put to so much trouble, as that, to comprehend what passes in their sight, they must have recourse to what was done, perhaps, ten or twenty years ago.

But there is another sort of relations, that is, of things happening in the action of the play, and supposed to be done behind the scenes; and this is many times both convenient and beautiful; for by it the French avoid the tumult to which we are subject in England, by representing duels, battles, and the like; which renders our stage too like the theatres where they fight prizes. For what is more ridiculous than to represent an army with a drum and five men behind it; all which the hero of the other side is to drive in before him; or to see a duel fought, and one slain with two or three thrusts of the foils, which we know are so blunted, that we might give a man an hour to kill another in good earnest with them? [Dryden, *Essay of Dramatic Poetry,* 1668.]

(*c*) Of all intellectual power, that of superiority to the fear of the invisible world is the most dazzling. . . . It can bribe us into a voluntary submission of our better knowledge, into suspension of all our judgment derived from constant experience, and enable us to peruse with the liveliest interest the wildest tales of ghosts, wizards, genii, and secret talismans. On this propensity, so deeply rooted in our nature, a specific *dramatic* probability may be raised by a true poet, if the whole of his work be in harmony: a dramatic probability, sufficient for dramatic pleasure, even when the component characters and incidents border on impossibility. The poet does not require us to be awake and believe; he solicits us only to yield ourselves to a dream; and this too with our eyes open, and with our judgment *perdue* behind the curtain, ready to awaken us at the first motion of our will: and meantime, only, not to disbelieve. [Coleridge, *Biographia Literaria,* 1817.]

(*d*) (*i*) We should try, as far as we can, to make up our shortcomings; and that to this end, instead of always fixing our thoughts upon the points in which our literature, and our intellectual life generally, are strong, we should, from time to time, fix them upon those in which they are weak, and so learn to perceive clearly what we have to amend.

(*ii*) Excellence is not common and abundant; on the contrary, as the Greek poet long ago said, excellence dwells among rocks hardly accessible, and a man must almost wear his heart out before he can reach her. Whoever talks of excellence as common and abundant, is on the way to lose all right standard of excellence. And when the right standard of excellence is lost, it is not likely that much which is excellent will be produced. . . . To our English race an inadequate sense for perfection of work is a real danger, the discipline of respect for a high and flawless excellence is peculiarly needed by us. [Matthew Arnold, *Essays in Criticisms,* 1865 and 1888.]

(*e*) . . . To make a child, now swaddled, to proceed
Man, and then shoot up, in one beard, and weed,
Past three score years; or, with three rusty swords,
And help of some few foot-and-half-foot words,
Fight over York, and Lancaster's long jars,
And in the tiring-house brings wounds, to scars.
He rather prays, you will be pleased to see
One such to-day, as other plays should be;
Where neither chorus wafts you o'er the seas;
Nor creaking throne comes down, the boys to please;
Nor nimble squib is seen, to make a feard
The gentlewomen; nor rolled bullet heard
To say, it thunders; nor tempestuous drum
Rumbles, to tell you when the storm doth come;
But deeds, and language, such as men do use:
And persons, such as comedy would choose,
When she would show an image of the times,

And sport with human follies, not with crimes.
[B. Jonson, Preface to *Every Man in his Humour*, 1598.]

5. How does Sidney answer these attacks on the Stage?
   (a) The best play you can pick out is but a mixture of good and evil, how can it be then the schoolmistress of life? The beholding of troubles and miserable slaughters that are in tragedies drive us to immoderate sorrow, heaviness, womanish weeping and mourning whereby we become lovers of dumps and lamentation, both enemies to fortitude. Comedies so tickle our senses with a pleasanter vein, that they make us lovers of laughter and pleasure, without any mean, both foes to temperance. What schooling is this?. [S. Gosson, *Playes compiled in Five Actions*, 1582.]
   (*b*) . . . Neither in polity nor in religion they [*plays*] are to be suffered in a Christian commonwealth, specially being of that frame and matter as usually they are, containing nothing but profane fables, lascivious matters, cozening devices, and scurrilous behaviours, which are so set forth as that they move wholly to imitation, and not to the avoiding of those faults and vices which they represent. [A letter from the Lord Mayor and Aldermen to the Privy Council, 1597].
   (*c*) O that men endued with reason, ennobled with religion; with immortal souls: fit only for the noblest, heavenliest, sublimest, and divinest actions, should ever be so desperately besotted as to waste their precious time upon such vain, such childish, base, ignoble pleasures [as *plays],* which can no way profit soul or body, Church or State; nor yet advance their temporal, much less their spiritual and eternal good, which they should ever seek. [Prynne, *Histrionmastix*, 1633.]
6. What words of Sidney's do these passages from Shakespeare recall? Would Sidney have modified his opinions had he known Shakespeare's plays?

(a) This castle hath a pleasant seat; the air
Nimbly and sweetly recommends itself
Unto our gentle senses.

[*Macbeth.*]

(*b*) **Richard.** Barkloughly Castle calls they this at hand?
Aum. Yea, my lord. How brooks your Grace the air,
After your late tossing on the breaking seas?

[*Richard II.*]

(*c*) And so our scene must to the battle fly;
Where,—O for pity,—we shall much disgrace,
With four or five most vile and ragged foils,
Right ill disposed in brawl ridiculous,
The name of Agincourt.

[*Henry V.*]

(*d*) Impute it not a crime
To me or my swift passage, that I slide
O'er sixteen years.

[*A Winter's Tale.*]

(e) **Macbeth.** Wherefore was that cry?
Seton. The Queen, my lord, is dead.

[*Macbeth.*]

7. Give other examples of parts of Shakespeare's plays which are apparently condemned by Sidney's criticism. Would Sidney be right to condemn them?
8. Give examples from your own reading of 'delight without Laughter.'

III

1. What would Jonson have to say about the length of such modern works as *Back to Methuselah* and *The Forsyte Saga*?
2. What balance does Jonson strike between Rules and Freedom to Experiment?
3. Find passages in Extract (*b*) which throw light on the exact meaning of the italicised words in this section of the Prologue to *Volpone, The Fox*.

   "And so presents quick comedy *refined*
   As *best* critics have designed
   The laws of time, place, persons he observeth,
   From no *needful* rule he swerveth."

4. What parts of Extract (*b*) suggest that Jonson would have enjoyed Mr. Guy Boas's lines on Shakespeare sitting for a Civil Service Examination?

   "The English papers of that year
   Contained a question on *King Lear*
   Which Shakespeare answered very badly—
   Because he hadn't studied Bradley."

5. "To judge of poets is only the faculty of poets." Does this mean that only novelists are qualified to judge novels, and that a novelist's criticism of a novel can be judged only by a man who is both novelist and critic of novels? Or was the man on surer ground who claimed that he was a better judge of an egg than the hen or "maker"?
6. Why was it a greater achievement to give a critical account of Shakespeare before 1637 than in 1665?
7. If Shakespeare had been able to read this account of himself, and had quoted from *Julius Cœsar*:

   Brutus. I do not like your faults.
   Cassius. A friendly eye could never see such faults.

   What would Jonson have answered?

8. In *Julius Cæsar* instead of "Cæsar never did wrong but with just cause," we now read:

   Know, Cæsar doth not wrong, nor without cause
   Will he be satisfied?"

   What may we conclude?

9. What points in (*b*) are illustrated and emphasised by the following words of Jonson himself?

   [Mitis has asked if the laws of comedy have been observed: Cordatus fails to see their necessity.]

   Cordatus, If these laws had been delivered to us *ab initio,* and in their present state and perfection, there had been some reason for obeying their powers . . . yet how is the face of it [*comedy*] changed since [Aristophanes], in Menander. . . . Plautus and the rest! who have utterly excluded the chorus, altered the property of the persons, their names and natures, and augmented it with all liberty, according to the elegancy and disposition of those times wherein they wrote. I see not then, but we shall enjoy the same licence, or free power to illustrate and heighten our invention, as they did; and not to be tied to those strict and regular forms which the niceness of a few, who are nothing but form, would thrust upon us. *[Every Man Out of his Humour*— Preface.]

10. To what extent would Jonson have agreed with the following?—

    (*a*) The drama's laws the drama's patrons give.

    (*b*) That pathetic faith which all Americans have in the power of professors to make an author of a man after twenty lessons in the craft of letters, caused him to spend a year at Harvard in taking the Drama Course. He had not yet realised what he was soon to realise, that every dramatist of quality makes his own technique. Whatever he learned during his year at Harvard he took pains to discard. If he knows anything of the rules of dramatic construction, as laid down by all the authorities from

Aristotle to William Archer and Professor G. P. Baker, he has carefully concealed his knowledge and written his plays as if he had none. . . . Aristotle would turn in his grave if he could hear of Mr. O'Neill's tricks with technique, but he might be induced to pardon them by the fact that they are extraordinarily successful. His plays, in short, are new adventures. [St. John Ervine.]

(*c*) . . . or whether the rules of Aristotle herein [*in epics*] are strictly to be kept, or nature to be followed, which in them that know art, and use judgment, is no transgression, but an enriching of art. [Milton, *The Reason of Church Government*, 1642.]

IV

1. "Almost every speech earns its position thrice over—explains something past, expresses somebody's character, and helps the action on" (C. E. Montague on J. M. Synge). To what extent is rhymed verse an obstacle to the second achievement?
2. "In his mouth the French dramatic couplet. . . was a thing, transfigured. Not that its own build and movement, so jolt some or jig-jog to some foreign ears, were disguised. They were revelled in, joyously championed. He practised on the verse a kind of double magic. First, he shed over the stiff-seeming lines such colour, diversity, warmth, colloquial quickness, that hearers, to whom these French Alexandrines had seemed to fall far short of human vivacity, half wondered whether perhaps the use of rhymed couplets was what human speech, in its longing for heightened expression at crises of feeling, had really been groping for always till now" (C. E. Montague on Coquelin). In view of this, to what extent does the writer's choice of means of expression (prose, blank-verse, rhymed verse) depend on the actor's ability? To what extent does it help to answer Desmond MacCarthy's question, "In his [Shakespeare's] day verse-drama was a living form. If he were re-born to-day, are you sure he would use it?"
3. "It is nearly impossible to permit persons moving on the intimately realistic settings of the modern stage to speak in verse." Why?
4. What would Dryden say to the following, from the Journal of Arnold Bennett?—

   "Stage Society in the afternoon. 'Good Friday,' by Masefield. A terribly dull and portentous thing in rhyme. I was most acutely bored. I found that all the élite said they liked the damned thing."
5. What experiments in verse-drama have been made by the following, and with what success?—

T. S. Eliot, G. Bottomley, W. B. Yeats, L. Macneice, W. H. Auden and C. Isherwood.

6. What hints of the influence of Dryden's example in writing plays in rhymed verse can be seen in Milton's Preface to *Paradise Lost* (1667)?—

   "Rime . . . but the invention of a barbarous age to set off wretched matter and lame metre; graced indeed since by the use of some famous modern poets, carried away by custom, but much to their own vexation, hindrance, and constraint, to express many things otherwise, and for the most part worse, than else they would have expressed them. . . Long since our best English tragedies [have rejected rhyme] as a thing of itself, to all judicious ears, trivial and of no true musical delight; which consists only in apt numbers, fit quantity of syllables, and the sense variously drawn out from one verse into another, not in the jingle sound of like endings. This neglect then of rime . . . is to be esteemed an example set, the first in English, of ancient liberty recovered to heroic poem from the troublesome and modern bondage of riming."

7. Give examples of Dryden's use of homely illustrations.
8. What claims does Lisideius seem to have made for the superiority of French drama? Which claims does Neander allow?
9. What is the longest speech in a modern play? Is it justified?
10. Give a good example from Shakespeare of "the chace of wit." What dramatists since Dryden have made good use of it?
11. Give instances of plays in which it is not easy to say which is the main character *(e.g.,* Galsworthy's *Strife).*
12. A remark of Dryden might be quoted to praise the modern play of crime or detection. Which?
13. Why are the plays of Shakespeare and Fletcher said to be irregular in contrast with Ben Jonson's?
14. What precisely is the meaning of "luckily" in the praise of Shakespeare?

V

(*a*)

1. Where watches disagree, Greenwich Mean Time can be referred to. To what standard can we refer when judgments differ?
2. Why must a critic know his own limitations?

(*b*)

3. What meaning does Pope attach to "wit"?
4. What importance does Pope attach to Restraint?
5. How does Criticism act as "the Muses' handmaid"?
6. What important lesson is to be learned from "young Maro"?
7. When is breaking the rules permissible?
8. Compare Wordsworth's confession of the "pastime to be bound/Within the Sonnet's scanty plot of ground." with Pope's theories of Restraint.
9. Would Pope agree with these statements by Max Beerbohm?—

   The artist presents his ideas in the finest, strictest form, paring, whittling, and polishing. In reading his finished work, none but a few persons note his artistic skill, or take pleasure in it for its own sake. Yet it is this very skill which enables reviewers to read his work with pleasure. To a few persons, artistic skill is in itself delightful, insomuch that they tend to overrate its importance, neglecting the matter for the form. Art, in a writer, is not everything. Indeed, it implies a certain limitation. If a list of consciously artistic writers were drawn up one would find that most of them were lacking in great force of intellect or of emotion; that their intellects were restricted, their emotions not very strong. Writers of enormous vitality never are artistic: they cannot pause, they must always be moving swiftly forwards.
10. What light is thrown on Pope's ideas of Imitation, Nature, and Rules by his remarks on Shakespeare?

(*a*) "The poetry of Shakespeare was inspiration indeed: he is not so much an imitator, as an instrument of Nature; and 'tis not so just to say that he speaks from her, as that she speaks through him.

"His characters are so much Nature herself that it is a sort of injury to call them by so distant a name as copies of her."

(*b*) "To judge . . . of Shakespeare by Aristotle's rules, is like trying a man by the laws of one country, who acted under those of another."

(*c*) What lines suggest that verse which does not violate any rules may still fail to be poetry?

11. What lines does this recall? [*of a Genius*], "He cannot at first discover it any other way than by giving way to that prevalent propensity which renders him the more liable to be mistaken. The only method he has, is to make the experiment by writing and appealing to the judgment of others." [Pope.]
12. From (*c*) choose the best (*a*) simile, (*b*) metaphor, (*c*) example of movement fitting sense.
13. "No criticism can be instructive which descends not to particulars, and is not full of examples and illustrations." Does Pope pass Hume's test?
14. Why should De Quincey (1785-1859) describe the *Essay on Criticism* as a series of commonplaces "the most mouldy with which criticism has baited its rat-traps"?

VI

(*a*) Taste

1. In what ways does Addison recall Pope's comparison of watches and judgments?
2. What is the accepted standard by which a reader can test the soundness of his taste? Is this a feature peculiar to Addison's age or one common to all ages?
3. Colour-blind people will declare that what is accepted as green is another colour. How can this be applied to the question of taste?
4. In speaking of the specific qualities of authors, why did Addison confines himself to examples from the classics?
5. What meaning does Addison attach to 'polite'?
6. Attempt a definition of "masterpiece" based on Addison's remarks.
7. Give instances from your own experience of (*a*) discovering new beauties on a second or later reading; (*b*) gaining new insight into an author by sharing your discoveries with another reader.
8. What instance from English literature might now be given of a group of writers of the first rank, who were friends and contemporaries?
9. What importance does Addison attach to rules?
10. What are Addison's ideas on (*a*) the aims, (*b*) the necessary training, (c) the test of a good critic?

(*b*) Pastoral Poetry

1. Could this be classed as an example of Historical Criticism?
2. "It is not enough to write about the country," says Steele. What other qualifications are added by modern critics—such as Mr. Auden?
3. To whom is this addressed—writers or readers?
4. If pastorals lead us into a kind of fairy land, was Pope, in writing Pastorals, following Nature?

5. What is the attitude of modern short-story writers to the more unpleasant aspects of life?
6. To what extent are Steele's reasons for the appeal of pastorals true of all "escape literature"? Why are such writings considered dangerous to-day?
7. What do the following extracts add to Steele's account?—
   (*a*) ... Pastoral, that traditional idealization of the shepherd's life, which the imagination of the Renaissance poets, first on the Continent and then in England, had built up upon the eclogues of Theocritus and of Virgil, and upon certain *chansons* of love-adventure between knights and village maidens, typical of native French poetry. . . . It had proved singularly attractive to a literary instinct which already, in the rapidly growing London of the late sixteenth and early seventeenth centuries, was beginning to feel the irksomeness of cities. It is the poetry of the reaction from civilisation, [with a] tendency, intelligible enough if illusory, to exalt the simplicity and content of the meadows above the pomp's of mortal state.

   . . . Pastoral is never to be mistaken for a transcript of rural life. Its significance resides, not in any fidelity to the fact of the peasant, but in its relation to the state of mind of the world-wearied courtier or scholar, who writes it. [Sir E. K. Chambers, *Shakespeare: A Survey*.]

   (*b*) If it is true that there are books written to escape from the present moment, and its meannesses and its sordidity, it is certainly true that readers are familiar with a corresponding mood. To draw the blinds and shut the door, to muffle the noises of the street and shade the glare and flicker of its lights—that is our desire. . . . The life that we invent, the stories we tell, as we sink back with half-shut eyes and pour forth our irresponsible dreams, have perhaps some wild beauty; some eager energy; we often reveal in them the distorted image of what we soberly and secretly desire. Thus the *Arcadia*, by wilfully flouting all contact with the fact, gains another reality. [Virginia Woolf, *The Common Reader*.]

(*c*) Indeed, most of the occasional pastorals we have, are built upon one and the same plan. A shepherd asks his fellow, "Why he is so pale? if his favourite sheep has strayed? if his pipe be broken? or Phyllis un-kind?" He answers, "None of these misfortunes have befallen him, but one much greater, for Damon (or sometimes the god Pan) is dead." This immediately causes the other to make complaints, and call upon the lofty pines and silver streams to join the lamentation. While he goes on, his friend interrupts him and tells him that Damon lives, and shews him a track of light in the skies to confirm it; then invites him to chestnuts and cheese. Upon this scheme half the noble families in Great Britain have been comforted. [Steele, No. 30 of *The Guardian*.]

(*d*) The pastoral belongs not to an age of strong faith and rugged action, but rather to an age when faith has become uncertain and action hesitant or tortuous, an age when criticism comes to be applied to what seems a dissolute time, a time of vice and hypocrisy, a time which has lost its old ideals. [Havelock Ellis, *Impressions and Comments*.]

(*e*) In this poem there is nothing new, for there is no truth; there is no art, for there is nothing new. Its form is that of a pastoral; easy, vulgar, and therefore disgusting; whatever images it can supply are long ago exhausted; and its inherent improbability always forces dissatisfaction on the mind. [Dr. Johnson on *Lycidas*.]

(*c*) Tragi-comedy

1. To what extent is the love of a happy ending still alive?
2. Which does Addison think to be the stronger objection to the happy ending—that it is not true to life, *or* that it defeats the end of tragedy, to raise pity and terror?
3. Why does Addison plead that the author should be free to choose between a happy and an unhappy ending, but not free to experiment in combining mirth and sorrow?

4. What play of Shakespeare's might have been cited as an example of "skillful choice of an underplot"?
5. In what ways are the audiences responsible for "faults" in English tragedy?
6. To what extent would Addison have agreed with the following?—
   (*a*) Pity is but a short-lived passion. I hate to hear an actor mouthing trifles: neither startings, strainings, nor attitudes affect me, unless there be cause; after I have been once or twice deceived by these unmeaning alarms, my heart sleeps in peace, probably unaffected by the principal distress. There should be one great passion aimed at by the actor, as well as the poet; all the rest should be subordinate, and only contribute to make that the greater: if the actor, therefore, exclaims upon every occasion, in tones of despair, he attempts to move us too soon; he anticipates the blow; he ceases to affect, though he gains our applause. [Goldsmith, *Citizen of the World*, 1760.]
   (*b*) An injudicious poet who aims at loftiness runs easily into the swelling puffy style, because it looks like greatness. . . . I dare not answer for an audience, that they would not clap it on the stage: so little value there is to the common cry, that nothing but madness can please madmen, and a poet must be of a piece with the spectators to gain a reputation with them. [Dryden, Epistle Dedicatory to *The Spanish Friar.]*
   (*c*) . . . This time I satisfied my own humour, which was to tack two plays together; and to break a rule for the pleasure of variety. The truth is, the audiences are grown weary of continued melancholy scenes; and I dare venture to prophesy that few tragedies except those in verse shall succeed in this age if they are not lightened with a course of mirth. For the feast is too dull and solemn without the fiddles. But how difficult a task this is will soon be tried; for a several genius is required to either way; and, without both of 'em, a man, in my

opinion, is but half a poet for the stage. Neither is it so trivial an undertaking to make a tragedy end happily; for 'tis more difficult to save than 'tis to kill. The dagger and the cup of poison are always in a readiness; but to bring the action to the last extremity, and then by probable means to recover all, will require the art and judgment of a writer, and cost him many a pang in the performance. [Dryden, *Ibid.*]

(*d*) . . . (*the so-called "happy ending"*). For this is the happy ending dearest to the sanitarian—that known causes should not have their known effects; above all, that in fifth acts any leopards which gain the playgoer's regard should be left rigged out in snowy, curly lambswool, and nice Ethiopians go off at the end as blonds with straight, tow-coloured hair. [C. E. Montague, *Dramatic Values*.]

(*e*) Shakespeare's plays are not in the rigorous and critical sense either tragedies or comedies, but compositions of a distinct kind; exhibiting the real state of sublunary nature, which partakes of good and evil, joy and sorrow, mingled with endless variety of proportion and innumerable modes of combination; and expressing the course of the world, in which the loss of one is the gain of another; in which, at the same time, the reveller is hasting to his wine, and the mourner burying his friend; in which the malignity of one is sometimes defeated by the frolic of another; and many mischiefs and many benefits are done and hindered without design. . . .

Shakespeare has united the powers of exciting laughter and sorrow not only in one mind, but in one composition. Almost all his plays are divided between serious and ludicrous characters, and, in the successive evolutions of the design, sometimes produce seriousness and sorrow, and sometimes levity and laughter.

That this is a practice contrary to the rules of criticism will be readily allowed; but there is always an appeal open from criticism to nature. The end of writing is to instruct; the end of poetry is to instruct by pleasing. [Dr. Johnson, Preface to *Shakespeare*, 1765.]

(*f*) O it offends me to the soul, to hear a robustious periwig-pated fellow, tear a passion to tatters, to very rags, to split the ears of the groundlings: . . . I could have such a fellow whipped for o'erdoing termagant: it out-herods Herod. Pray you avoid it. . . . Suit the action to the word, the word to the action, with this special observance, that you o'erstep not the modesty of Nature; for anything so overdone is from the purpose of playing, whose end both at the first and now, was and is, to hold as 'twere the mirror up to Nature. [Hamlet's speech to the Players.]

VII

1. Are Dr. Johnson's statements ever unsupported by reason or illustration?
2. The first quotation should be the last but one of Section I. Justify placing it here.
3. Is there any evidence to support the suggestion that Boswell recorded these sayings not because they were great truths but because they came from a great man?
4. What is Dr. Johnson's attitude to (*a*) speakers who oppose him; (*b*) those who listen without taking part in the duels; (c) the general reading public?
5. Test Dr. Johnson's conversation by his own words: "Talking of conversation," he said, "there must, in the first place, be knowledge, there must be materials;— in the second place, there must be a command of words; —in the third place, there must be imagination, to place things in such views as they are not commonly seen in; —and in the fourth place, there must be presence of mind, and a resolution that is not to be overcome by failures."
6. "It (*a character in Shakespeare*) is generally a species." Explain.
7. To what extent is Johnson's formula for the routine method of planning the affairs of lovers true of (*a*) modern fiction; (*b*) modern films?
8. If Johnson does not like love to be the mainspring of the plot, what plays written since his day would be likely to please him?
9. Estimate Johnson's opinion of the annotated editions of your set books in English Literature.

VIII

1. In what ways is the familiar style a happy medium?
2. What exactly are Hazlitt's objections to (*a*) Dr. Johnson's style; (*b*) coining new words; (*c*) the theory that "the first word that occurs is always the best"; (*d*) archaic words and phrases; (*e*) current slang?
3. On what grounds does Hazlitt allow that use of archaic words to be a virtue in Lamb?
4. If the vulgar and the fashionable admire the gaudy style, what other classes are to be considered, and what other tribunals must the author consider?
5. What evidence is there of Hazlitt's familiarity with Shakespeare?
6. Apply Hazlitt's tests to the following passage by him:

   If, indeed, by a great poet, we mean one who gives the utmost grandeur to our conceptions of nature, or the utmost force to the passions of the heart, Pope was not in this sense a great poet; for the bent, the characteristic power of his mind, lay the clean contrary way; namely, in representing things as they appear to the indifferent observer, stripped of prejudice and passion, as in his Critical Essays; or in representing them in the most contemptible and insignificant point of view, as in his Satires; or in clothing the little with mock-dignity, as in his poems of Fancy; or in adorning the trivial incidents and familiar relations of life with the utmost elegance of expression, and all the flattering illusions of friendship, or self-love, as in his Epistles. He was not then distinguished as a poet of lofty enthusiasm, of strong imagination, with a passionate sense of the beauties of nature, or a deep insight into the workings of the heart; but he was a wit, and a critic, a man of sense, of observation, and the world, with a keen relish for the elegances of art, or of nature when embellished by art, a quick tact for propriety of thought and manners as established by the forms and customs of the society, a refined sympathy with the sentiments and habitudes of human life, as he felt them within the little circle of his family and his friends. He was, in a word, the poet, not of nature, but of Art. . . . The poet of nature is one who, from the elements of beauty, of power, and of passion in his own breast, sympathises with whatever is beautiful, and grand, and impassioned in nature, in its simple majesty, in its immediate appeal to the senses, to the thoughts and hearts of all men; so that the poet of nature, by the truth, and depth, and harmony of his mind, may be said to hold communion with the very soul of nature; to be identified with and to foreknow and to record the feelings of all men at all times and places, as they are liable to the same impressions; and to exert the same power over the minds of his readers, that nature does. He sees things in their eternal beauty, for he sees them as they are; he feels them in their universal interest, for he feels them as they affect the first principles of his and our common nature. Such was Homer, such was Shakespeare, whose works will last as long as nature, because they are a copy of the indestructible forms and everlasting impulses of nature, welling out from the bosom as from a perennial spring, or stamped upon the senses by the hand of their maker. The power of the imagination in them is the representative power of all nature. It has its centre in the human soul, and makes the circuit of the universe. [*Lectures on the English Poets.*]

7. Which sections of the following descriptions of a writer's style would meet with Hazlitt's approval?—
   (*a*) [*On Swift*]. His style is well-suited to his thoughts, which are never subtilised by nice disquisitions, decorated by sparkling conceits, elevated by ambitious sentences, or variegated by far-sought learning. He pays no court to the passions; he excites neither surprised nor admiration; he always understands himself: and his reader understands him: the peruser of Swift wants little previous knowledge: it will be sufficient that he is acquainted with common words and common things; he is neither required to mount elevations, nor to explore

profundities; his passage is always on a level, along solid ground, without asperities, without obstruction. [Dr. Johnson.]

(*b*) [*On Carlyle*]. . . . A style resembling either early architecture or utter dilapidation, so loose and rough it seemed; a wind-in-the-orchard style, that tumbles down here and there with an appreciable fruit with uncouth bluster; sentences without commencement running to abrupt endings and smoke, like waves against a sea-wall, learned dictionary words giving a hand to street-slang and accents falling on them haphazard like slant rays from driving clouds; all the pages in a breeze, the whole book producing a kind of electrical agitation in the mind and joints. [G. Meredith.]

(*c*) [*The ideal writer*]. He writes passionately, because he feels keenly; forcibly, because he conceives vividly; he sees too clearly to be vague; he is too serious to be otiose; he can analyse his subject, and therefore he is rich; he embraces it as a whole and in its parts, and therefore he is consistent; he has a firm hold of it, and therefore he is luminous. When his imagination wells up, it overflows in ornament; when his heart is touched, it thrills along his verse. He always has the right word for the right idea, and never a word too much. If he is brief, it is because few words suffice; when he is lavish of them, still each word has its mark, and aids, not embarrasses, the vigorous march of his elocution. He expresses what all feel, but all cannot say; and his sayings pass into proverbs among his people, and his phrases become household words and idioms of their daily speech, which is tessellated with the rich fragments of his language, as we see in foreign lands the marbles of Roman grandeur worked into the walls and palaces of modern palaces. [Cardinal Newman.]

IX

1. To what extent is Lamb in danger of accusing Shakespeare of not knowing his job?
2. What use does Lamb make of rhetorical questions— and hurrying on before you find a different answer from the one he intended?
3. What evidence is there of the liberties taken with Shakespeare's text?
4. How is it possible to act unless the actor is "thinking all the while of his own appearance"?
5. Give instances from your own experience of (*a*) changing your opinion of a character in a play after seeing an actor's interpretation; (*b*) annoyance or disgust when someone else's picture of a person (in a book illustration or on the screen) has differed from the one you have built up and cherished.
6. Answer Lamb's questions [of the physical properties of Garrick]:
   (*a*) "What have they to do with Hamlet? What have they to do with intellect?"
   (*b*) "What has the voice or the eye to do with such things" as the outbursts of Lear in the storm?
7. Did Shakespeare intend the spectator (*a*) to feel disgusted by Richard's crimes; (*b*) to feel that the crimes of Macbeth and Iago were "comparatively nothing"; (*c*) to find delight in the feeling of pain and uneasiness caused by seeing Macbeth about to murder Duncan?
8. Show that Lamb regards the intellect and taste of the average playgoer as greatly inferior to that of the average reader.
9. What would Lamb say to the following?—
   (*a*) Bibles should never be illustrated.
   (*b*) Much more than interpretation is asked of the actor. He has to *embody* the character.
   (*c*) Dramatic dialogue has two obvious ends, the telling of the story and the disclosure of character. But

there is another not so obvious; it must be made to stimulate our imagination and emotion.

(*d*) *King Lear* is too huge for the stage. . . . That which makes the *peculiar* greatness of *King Lear*—the immense scope of the work; the mass and variety of intense experience which it contains; the interpenetration of sublime imagination, piercing pathos, and humour almost as moving as the pathos; the vastness of the convulsion both of nature and of human passion; the vagueness of the scene where the action takes place, and of the movements of the figures which cross this scene; the strange atmosphere, cold and dark, which strikes on us as we enter this scene, enfolding those figures and magnifying their dim outlines like a winter mist; the half-realised suggestions of vast universal powers working in the world of individual fears and passions; all this interferes with dramatic clearness even when the play is read, and in the theatre not only refuses to reveal itself fully through the sense but seems to be almost in contradiction with their reports. [A. C. Bradley, *Shakespearean Tragedy*.]

(*e*) [*Of Irving*]. He took no interest in the drama as such: a play was to him a length of stuff necessary to his appearance on the stage, but so entirely subordinate to that consummation that it could be cut to his measure like a roll of cloth. . . . Even in his Shakespearean impostures (for such they were) there were unforgettable moments. But he composed his parts not only without the least consideration for the play as a whole, or even for the character as portrayed by the author (he always worked out some fancy of his own), but without any for the unfortunate actors whom he employed to support him. [G. B. Shaw.]

(*f*) Two of the prime cuts in the body of cant are the statements that Shakespeare did not mean his play of *King Lear* to be acted, and that it is in fact unactable. [Speaking of a performance in 1934.] . . . The philosophy of the play comes through as well as its poetry.

[James Agate.]

X

(*a*)

1. (*a*) What difference is made by substituting "vocabulary" for "language" in Wordsworth's statements?

   (*b*) Would Wordsworth agree with the following?— . . . I cut myself off from the use of *ere, o'er, well-nigh, what time, say not* (for *do not say),* because, though dignified, they neither belong to nor ever c[oul]d arise from, or be the elevation of, ordinary modern speech. For it seems to me that the poetical language of an age sh[oul]d be the current language heightened, to any degree heightened and unlike itself but not ... an obsolete one. This is Shakespeare's and Milton's practice and the want of it will be fatal to Tennyson's Idylls and plays, to Swinburne, and perhaps to Morris. [1879. G. M. Hopkins.]

2. The following passage explains Wordsworth's objections to figures of speech:

   Simile and metaphor, things unessential to poetry, were their [*18th-century poets*] great engrossing preoccupation, and were prized more in proportion as they were further fetched. They did not mean those accessorics to be helpful, to make their sense clearer or their conceptions more vivid; they hardly even meant them for ornament, or cared whether an image had any independent power to please; their objection was to startle and amuse by ingenuity a public whose one wish was to be startled and amused. [A. E. Housman, *The Name and Nature of Poetry,* 1935.]

   By objecting to figures of speech because of their abuse, in what ways was Wordsworth the poorer?

3. Which sections of the following offer a clue to Wordsworth's reasons for refraining from using "expressions . . . foolishly repeated by bad Poets"?

   In the main, conventions die of being used to death. Poets of low vitality ensconce themselves like hermit-crabs, generation after generation, in the cast-off shells of their ancestors.

Poetry, as the radicals react to it, is shackled by a mass of inherited conventions—dead rhymes, dead metres, dead diction, dead stock ideas. They would play the rôle of Perseus to a new Andromeda, and set the starry prisoner free. [J. L. Lowes, *Convention and Revolt,* 1930.]

4. In what ways does this differ from Wordsworth's statement of the approximation of the "language" of prose to that of verse?

Every man conversant with verse-writing knows, and knows by painful experience, that the familiar style is of all styles the most difficult to succeed in. To make verse speak the language of prose, without being prosaic, —to marshall the words of it in such an order as they might naturally take in falling from the lips of an extemporary speaker, yet without meanness, harmoniously, elegantly, and without seeming to displace a syllable for the sake of the rhyme, is one of the most arduous tasks a poet can undertake. [Cowper, Letter of 1782.]

(*b*)

5. Is Coleridge's *lingua communis* the same as the 'permanent speech' described in the following?—

If there be, what I believe there is, in every nation, a stile which never becomes obsolete, a certain mode of phraseology so consonant and congenial to the analogy and principles of its respective language as to remain settled and unaltered; this style is probably to be sought in the common intercourse of life, among those who speak only to be understood, without ambition or elegance. The polite are always catching modish innovations, and the learned depart from established forms of speech, in hope of finding or making better; those who wish for distinction forsake the vulgar, when the vulgar is right; but there is a conversation above grossness and below refinement, where propriety resides. [Dr. Johnson, *Preface to Shakespeare.*]

6. Can the language of rustics, or of any other class, be transferred to the drama without alteration, suppression, arrangement, or condensation?
7. Compare the following dicta of Coleridge with what he says in (b):
   (*i*) The collocation of words is so artificial in Shakespeare and Milton, that you may as well think of pushing a brick out of a wall with your forefinger, as attempt to remove a word out of any of their finished passages.
   (*ii*) The definition of good prose is—proper words in their proper places; of good verse—the most proper words in their proper places. The propriety is in either case relative. The words in prose ought to express the intended meaning, and no more; if they attract attention to themselves, it is, in general, a fault. In the very best styles, as Southey's, you read page after page, understanding the author perfectly, without once taking notice of the medium of communication;—it is as if he had been speaking to you all the while. But in verse you must do more;—there the words, the *media,* must be beautiful, and ought to attract your notice—yet not so much and so perpetually as to destroy the unity which ought to result from the whole poem. This is the general rule, but, of course, subject to some modifications, according to the different kinds of prose or verse. [*Table Talk.*]
8. How does Coleridge's idea of the "compact between the poet and the reader" differ from those expressed in the following passages?—
   (*i*) It is supposed, that by the act of writing in verse an Author makes a formal engagement that he will gratify certain known habits of association; that he not only thus apprises the Reader that certain classes of ideas and expressions will be found in his book, but that others will be carefully excluded. [Wordsworth, Preface to *Lyrical Ballads.*]
   (*ii*) If I have an experience of undisputed authenticity and importance to communicate, then the burden

of understanding it is on the reader, to whom I have fulfilled my responsibility by setting it down, in what seems to *me* the most exact and simplest possible terms. An authentic and important experience cannot be the slave of readers of unknown capacities for response. The best I can do for these readers is to occupy myself with the precision of my experience, to be "at home," so to write, should anyone call. The reader is in the position of calling on me, not of being called on by me. [Laura Riding.]

9. Does this coincide with Coleridge's conclusion?

   The diction of poetry includes every word that poetry can use. [J. L. Lowes.]

10. Give examples of the importance of associations recalled by words in poetry, as described by Coleridge, and by Joubert in the following:

    In the style of poetry, each word reverberates like the note of a well-tuned lyre, and always leaves behind it a multitude of vibrations.

11. How does "the second characteristic excellence" differ from Pope's, "What oft was thought but ne'er so well expressed"?
12. Distinguish "the obscurity of all good poetry" from "the obscurity of all new poetry."
13. What contribution do Coleridge's comparisons make?
14. Apply Coleridge's fuller expression of the distinction between Fancy and Imagination to that hinted at in the account of the "last excellence."

    . . . Such descriptions too often occasion in the mind of a reader, who is determined to understand his author, a feeling of labour, not very dissimilar to that with which he would construct a diagram, line by line, for a long geometrical proposition. It seems to be like taking the pieces of a dissected map out of its box. We first look at one part, then at another, then dove-tail them; and when the successive acts of attention have been completed, there is a retrogressive effort of mind to behold it as a whole. The poet should paint to imagination, not to the fancy.

15. What different meaning from that used by Coleridge has "poetry" in "The preface to Bunyan's *Pilgrim's Progress* is verse, but it is not poetry. The body of the work is poetry, but it is not prose"? [Samuel Butler, Notebooks.]
16. Does this account of poetry in *Table Talk* differ from anything in Section (*d*)?

    I think nothing can be added to Milton's definition or rule of poetry,—that it ought to be simple, sensuous, and impassioned; that is to say, single in conception, abounding in sensible images, and informing them all with the spirit of the mind.
17. Would Coleridge approve of the anthologist's habit of taking a section of a longer poem and printing it as a whole poem? [*e.g.*, Mrs. Barbauld's "Life! I know not what thou art," in *The Golden Treasury*.]
18. Compare the following with Coleridge's account of the pleasure given by poetry:

    To read a poem for the sake of the pleasure which will ensue if it is successfully read is to approach it in an inadequate attitude. Obviously, it is the poem in which we should be interested, not in a by-product of having managed successfully to read it. [I. A. Richards, *Principles of Literary Criticism.* He gives as an analogy the noise of a motor-cycle—the by-product, not the aim of the activity in the course of which it arises.]
19. Is the importance attached to music in poetry, shown in (*d*) and in "To please me, a poem must be either music or sense" [*Table Talk*], a feature of Coleridge's day or of all times?
20. It is said that every man could write one novel based on his own character and experiences. Would Coleridge agree?
21. Which of Jane Austen's novels gives the best example of her aloofness? Have any modern novelists this gift?
22. What reference to the language of poetry is made in the description of the four distinguishing marks of poetic power?

XI

(*a*)

1. In what specialised sense does Keats use 'Sensations'?
2. What parallel is suggested by the closing lines of the "Ode to a Grecian Urn"?—

   Beauty is truth, truth beauty,—that is all
   Ye know on earth, and all ye need to know.

(*b*)

3. Just why would Keats consider Wordsworth's aim wrong?— Every great Poet is a Teacher: I wish either to be considered as a Teacher, or as nothing.
4. Would Shelley be criticised by Keats for his avowed aim in the Preface to *The Revolt of Islam*?

   I have sought to enlist the harmony of metrical language, the ethereal combinations of the fancy, the rapid and subtle transitions of human passion, and all those elements which essentially compose a Poem, in the cause of a liberal and comprehensive morality. . . . I have made no attempt to recommend the motives which I would substitute for those at present governing mankind, by methodical and systematic argument. I would only awaken the feelings, so that the reader should see the beauty of true virtue, and be incited to those enquiries which have led to my moral and political creed. . . . The Poem therefore ... is narrative, not didactic.

(*c*)

5. Do these statements by Keats in other letters blend with the main ideas of this and other sections?—
   (*i*) Fine writing is next to fine doing, the top thing in the world.
   (*ii*) I look upon fine phrases as a lover.

(*iii*) He [*Shelley*] describes what he sees: I describe what I imagine. Mine, is the harder task.

(*d*)

6. What point is illustrated by this quotation from Keats's letter of 1817?
   The excellence of every art is its intensity, capable of making all disagreeable evaporate, from their being in close relationship with Beauty and Truth. Examine *King Lear,* and you will find this exemplified throughout.
7. Would Keats agree that poetry is neither moral nor immoral?
8. Compare these dicta on poetry with those of Keats:
   (*i*) Poetry, with its discoveries of the beautiful in familiar matters, its pictures and decisions in a few words, its singular command of 'the best words in the best order,' it's unexpected yet appropriate comparisons, its musical intricacy without effort, its aspiring constancy without sermonizings. . . . [Edmund Blunden.]
   (*ii*) A poem should not mean but be. [A. MacLeish.]
   (*iii*) What shall we require of poetry? Delight, music, subtlety of thought, a world of the heart's desire, fidelity to comprehensible experience, a glimpse through magic casements, profound wisdom?
   We require the highest. All that can be demanded of any spiritual activity of man we must demand of poetry. [J. M. Murry.]
   (*iv*) Verse is Words put into a Wanton Posture. [Rev. John Edwards.]
   (*v*) There is the minor poet, the major poet, and the pure poet. The first two are to be considered as in their degrees to and from each other, but the third is dimensionless: it is not referable to either of these, nor included within the terms of the greater and the less. Each of the inseparable two are calculable in terms of the gravity, or lack of it, of their subject-matter, nor is

subject-matter at all to be eluded by them. The third is seen to be getting along quite prettily without a subject-matter, without an intellection, and without, as it were, a passion: certainly without any lay emotion.

It is passionate and rational indeed, and is, perhaps, nothing else: but it is passionate in another mode, is rational in another way—and is satisfying without reference to these. The word "magic" has been contrived as upon this art: this word indicates—another, an unknown, a greatly desirable. It, like life, has, perhaps, no other function but to be desirable, and satisfying. [James Stephens.]

XII

1. What difference is made by this qualification?—"But for supreme poetical success more is required than the powerful applications of ideas to life; it must be an application under the conditions fixed by the laws of poetic truth and poetic beauty. Those laws fix as an essential condition . . . high seriousness; — the high seriousness which comes from absolute sincerity." [This Arnold fails to find in Burns' lines:

   To make a happy fire-side clime
     To weans and wife,
   That's the true pathos and sublime
     Of human life

   because "he is not speaking to us from these depths (*the innermost soul of the genuine Burns*), he is more or less preaching."]
2. What answer to this criticism of Keats by Arnold could be found in Keats's Letters?

   A merely sensuous man cannot either by promise or performance be a very great poet, because poetry interprets life, and so large and noble a part of life is outside of such a man's ken—we cannot but look for signs in him of something more than sensuousness, for signs of character and virtue.
3. Arnold seems to admit Wordsworth, Milton, and Shakespeare to the select class of poets of the highest class, and to reject Keats and Burns. What other poets do you think would really satisfy Arnold?
4. Name some poems that have given you continued satisfaction and deep pleasure and yet do not seem to offer any criticism of life.
5. Does Arnold's definition of *grand style* agree with his statements in this extract—"the grand style arises in poetry when a noble nature, poetically gifted, treats with simplicity or severity a serious subject"?

6. Byron, in *Hints from Horace,* says of plays:

   The moral's scant—but that may be excused,
   Men go not to be lectured, but amused.

   . . . Plays make mankind no better, and no worse.

   Suggest the attitude Arnold would take.

7. Wordsworth hoped that the destiny of his poems would be—"to console the afflicted; to add sunshine to daylight, by making the happy happier; to teach the young and the gracious of every age to see, to think, and feel, and therefore to become more actively and securely virtuous."

   Is such a worthy *aim* essential for poetry to earn the right to be admitted to Arnold's highest class?

8. What examples of 'poetry of revolt against moral ideas' and of 'poetry of indifference towards moral ideas' existed in Arnold's day? What subsequent examples might be added?

9. What exactly is added by Mr. I. A. Richards in the following quotation from *The Principles of Literary Criticism*?

   For the arts are inevitably and quite apart from any intentions of the artist an appraisals of existence. Matthew Arnold, when he said that poetry is a criticism of life, was saying something so obvious that it is constantly overlooked. The artist is concerned with the record and perpetuation of the experiences which seem to him most worth having. . . . He is also the man, who is most likely to have experiences of value to record. He is the point at which the growth of the mind shows itself.

XIII

1. "The materials of fiction being human nature and circumstances"—are, then, the materials of drama the same?
2. Why does Hardy rule out from his discussion the question of planning a story?
3. What is meant by being "more truthful than truth"?
4. Who are "the van-couriers of taste," and why should creativeness have ceased to satisfy them?
5. Discuss from your own reading Mr. Desmond MacCarthy's statement: "Invention seems rather more common in novelists who make no pretence to be artists or critics of life; and the result is that their novels are often better than those of writers endowed with æsthetic sensibility, ideas and psychological insight."
6. Explain the force of the words in italics:
   (*a*) Realism is an *artificiality distilled* from the fruits of closest observation.
   (*b*) A keen eye to the superficial does not imply a sensitiveness to the *intrinsic*.
7. What allowances are made for possible change in and development of the novel?
8. What is the difference between a broadcast description of a man wanted by the police and a novelist's picture of a character?
9. What is the writer's attitude to the "trade of story-telling," and how is it revealed?
10. Compare the following dicta by living writers—names are deliberately withheld—with corresponding sections of Hardy's Essay:
    (*a*) Your history and your novel are alike imaginative reconstructions of reality, and that is their common glory. No records will convince us, unless the heart is convinced.

(*b*) The art of the novelist does not consist in descriptions so much as in making statements in the right order.

(*c*) Fiction is digested experience, and a great novel is the reflection of a great man's sense of the world and of the people in it.

(*d*) People who are anxious to shine can never tell a plain story.

(*e*) A novel . . . should be a little history of humanity, cunningly selected to betray our essential attributes, and a plot is its vitality.

(*f*) We go to the novel to enlarge our knowledge of human nature and to enlarge it not only by unusual and amusing but more especially by significant experiences.

(*g*) We must be made to feel that the vivacity and oddity of things are not the whole of them, and that some experiences count for more than others because they strike on deeper emotions.

(*h*) By 'great' when applied to a novelist, I should have meant to suggest that the writer . . . was chiefly concerned with some of the most important things in life, and had a power of conveying his preoccupation with them adequate to their importance.

(*i*) An artist is one who puts in what belongs to his subject no matter how bad it is, and leaves out what doesn't belong to it no matter how good it is.

(*j*) We mean by it ['*materialist*'] that they write of unimportant things; that they spend immense skill and immense industry in making the trivial and the transitory appear the true and the enduring.

(*k*) So much of the enormous labour of proving the solidity, the likeness to life, of the story is not merely labour thrown away but labour misplaced to the extent of obscuring and blotting out the light of the conception.

(*l*) The story-teller arranges life to suit his purpose. He follows a design in the mind, leaving out this and changing that, he distorts facts to his advantage, according to his plan, and when he attains his object, it is a work of art.

11. How would Hardy's idea of a good novel differ from this?—
One would say that being good means representing virtuous and aspiring characters placed in prominent positions; another would say that it depends on a 'happy ending,' on a distribution at the last, of prizes, pensions, husbands, wives, babies, millions, appended, paragraphs, and cheerful remarks. Another still would say that it means being full of incident and movement, so that we shall still wish to see who was the mysterious stranger, and if the stolen will was ever found, and shall not be distracted from this pleasure by any tiresome analysis or 'description.'

[Henry James.]

XIV

1. In what sense is Galsworthy using the word 'morals'?
2. Does the work of the pure artist provide an exception to Arnold's 'criticism of life' theory?
3. Can you suggest an example of a writer, who is as near to being 'pure moralist' as Conrad is to being 'pure artist'?
4. To what extent is moralist and artist balanced in G. B. Shaw? Does this account for his popularity to-day?
5. With which of these two statements would Galsworthy agree?—
   (*a*) The test of a work of art is whether it communicates certain emotions, which have a moral value, to the ordinary unsophisticated man. (Tolstoy's theory.)
   (*b*) A work of art is justified of itself without any consideration of moral effect.
6. If two writers, A. (artist) and M. (moralist), write about a time and place with revolting customs, how would they betray their attitudes?
7. In what way is it possible to agree that Shakespeare is dateless, and yet to maintain that he is a great moralist?
8. In what ways does this tally with Galsworthy's theories?
   That our plays ought not to take sides in politics or other questions of the day is one of the things that people daily say, not knowing what they say, nor trying to know. Some plays ought to, and others ought not. It depends upon what makes their authors write best, the advocate's heat or the bystander's curiosity. [C. E. Montague.]
9. What superiority of the artist over the moralist in affecting the reader's attitude to problems of conduct and conscience is indicated by the following?—
   (*a*) [*Of Ibsen*]. He simply represented things as he saw them and left people to form what judgments they might. ... He offered only to help them to see more clearly the situation. [C. E. Montague.]
   (*b*) In the best art we perceive persons, things, and situations more clearly than in life and as though they were in

some way more real than realities themselves. [Aldous Huxley.]

10. Does 'propagandist' here mean the same as 'moralist'?—
If you feel impelled by the appearance of the world to say something about it, whether in an ode, or a symphony, or as the Chinese potter did with his conventional blue and white hawthorn design of breaking ice and white petals, to show the spring, then you must be a propagandist. [H. M. Tomlinson.]

11. What do these statements by Galsworthy reveal of the proportions in which artist and moralist combine in him?—
(*a*) It can be understood how modern artist, strongly and pitifully impressed by the circling pressure of modern environments, predisposed to the naturalistic method, and with something in him of the satirist, will neither create characters seven or even six feet high, nor write plays detached from the movements and problems of his times. He is not conscious, however, of any desire to solve these problems in his plays, or to effect direct reforms. His only ambition in drama, as in his other work, is to present truth as he sees it, and, gripping with it his readers or his audience, to produce in them a sort of mental and moral ferment, whereby vision may be enlarged, imagination livened, and understanding promoted. [Preface to plays in Manaton edition.]
(*b*) I am not a reformer—only a painter of pictures, a maker of things—as sincerely as I know how—imagined out of what I have seen and felt. The sociological character of my plays arises from the fact that I do not divorce creation from life; that, living and moving, feeling and seeing amongst real life, I find myself moved now and then—not deliberately and consciously—to present to myself the types, and ideas, and juxtapositions of life that impinge on my consciousness, and clarify it all out in the form of a picture.
(*c*) I try to be and to keep in the middle of things, and to strike at what seems to me redundant and extravagant on either side. This is what I humbly think is the function of art in its negative and satiric form.

XV

1. "Critical remarks are not easily understood without examples," says Dr. Johnson. Estimate the value of the quotations employed by Mr. Eliot.
2. Which of the characteristics of metaphysical poets, often mistermed 'peculiarities,' are claimed to be characteristics of all great poets?
3. Why did "the attempt to define metaphysical poetry by its faults" fail?
4. "We dwell with satisfaction upon the poet's difference from his predecessors, especially his immediate predecessors; we endeavour to find something that can be isolated in order to be enjoyed. Whereas if we approach a poet without this prejudice we shall often find that not only the best, but the most individual parts of his work may be those in which the dead poets, his ancestors, assert their immortality most vigorously." [T. S. Eliot, *Tradition and the Individual Talent.*] What echo of this is found in the present essay?
5. "The poetry of a people takes its life from the people's speech and in turn gives life to it; and represents its highest point of consciousness, its greatest power and its most delicate sensibility." What meaning does Mr. Eliot attach to 'sensibility' in this quotation and in the essay?
6. Donne is described as an intellectual poet, Tennyson as a reflective one. To which of the two kinds of poetry does modern verse lean?
7. Elsewhere Mr. Eliot refers to Milton as "our greatest master of the *artificial* style," and says Dryden's "*style* (vocabulary, syntax, and order of thought) is in a high degree natural." What do you consider to be 'the poetic functions whose absence was concealed by the magnificence of the performance of certain poetic functions'?
8. "The possible interests of a poet are unlimited." Illustrate this from post-war poetry.

9. "It appears likely that poets in our civilisation, as it exists at present, must be *difficult.*" (*a*) What are Mr. Eliot's reasons for thinking so? (*b*) What is the importance of the qualification "as it exists at present"? (*c*) If this is true, is any change in the readers of poetry likely to follow?
10. In speaking of Milton's disregard of the soul, what meaning does he attach to "soul"?
11. If it can be said that Mr. Eliot speaks as one with authority, what gives him the authority?
12. What defence does Mr. Eliot offer against these criticisms of metaphysical poets?—
    (*a*) The mind in perusing a work overstocked with wit, is fatigued and disgusted with the constant endeavour to shine and surprise. [Hume.]
    (*b*) It is all highly *irritant* poetry, disquieted and disquieting; its chief deficiency is that of any simple and direct feeling for the beauty of the world. Even the beauty of women is not seen simply; the restless refining intellect as it were pounces on the vision and dissipates it in a thousand reasoning's. [O. Elton.]
13. Compare the following with the relevant sections of Mr. Eliot's essay:
    (*a*) A phrase of poetry drops into the mind like a stone into a pool. The waves go out and out in expanding circles. How soon will they break on a confining shore? It depends on the native abilities and the acquired culture of each individual mind. A dull, uneducated Spirit is a mere well, narrow between walls; but in a lively and cultivated mind the waves can run on for the imaginative equivalent of miles and hours. [Aldous Huxley.]
    (*b*) The words are cut to the quick, the thought goes like a weaver's shuttle. [O. Elton on Donne.]
    (*c*) The rising of emotion in a writer invariably reveals to him many unexpected connections between things; and because it is itself a symptom of emotion, this surprising agility of mind engenders an emotion in us. [D. MacCarthy.]

14. Apply the following statements by Mr. Eliot to this essay:
    (*a*) From time to time, every hundred years or so, it is desirable that some critic shall appear to review the past of our literature, and set the poets and the poems in a new order. The task is not one of revolution but of readjustment. . . . The majority of critics can be expected only to parrot the opinions of the last master of criticism; among more independent minds a period of destruction, of preposterous over-estimation, and of successive fashions takes place, until a new authority comes to introduce some order. . . . Hence, each new master of criticism performs a useful service merely by the fact that his errors are of a different kind from the last.
    (*b*) When the critics are themselves poets, it may be suspected that they have formed their critical statements with a view to justifying their poetic practice.
    (*c*) Each age demands different things from poetry, though its demands are modified, from time to time, by what some new poet has given. So our criticism, from age to age, will reflect the things that the age demands.

XVI

1. Compare this statement by Hopkins with the first sentence: I sometimes wonder at this ["*that there may be genius uninformed by character*"] in a man like Tennyson: his gift of utterance is truly golden, but goes further home and you come to thoughts commonplace and wanting in nobility.
2. What light is thrown on the "sincerity" of the first sentence by these tributes to Hopkins?—
   (*a*) A Catholic of the most scrupulous strictness, he could nevertheless see the Holy Spirit in all goodness, truth, and beauty. [Patmore.]
   (*b*) Hopkins was always remembered by all who met him as essentially a priest, a deep and prayerful religious. With the fine uncompromising courage of his initial conversion, he pursued his never-ending quest after spiritual perfection. [Father Lahey.]
3. Would Hopkins or Read agree with the following?—
   (*a*) The fundamental, the guiding principle in English poetry has always been: you must counterpoint to avoid monotony, but you must not silence the pattern. You can only work within limits, and if you go beyond them, the result is prose. [G. M. Young.]
   (*b*) The rhythmical beauty of verse lies in its subtle variation from a strict metrical basis, in its avoidance, by the shifting or resolution of its normal stresses, of a regularity which would soon become intolerably monotonous. Its aim is thus to achieve the greatest elasticity of movement compatible with a strict sense of form. The art of the poet consists in his power to do this, and to do it in such a way as to create a music not only in itself beautiful, but peculiarly expressive of the emotion which he has to convey, just as the musical composer may take a melody and express his moods in the variations he plays upon it. But the poet's difficulty is greater than the musician's, in that the syllables of

his words, which are the equivalent in poetry of the musician's notes, are not mere notes in a scale, but are essential parts of the intellectual symbols which convey his thought. [E. de Selincourt.]

4. How far do these quotations from Hopkins's letters answer the charges that his verse is lawless or that it is a clean break with tradition?—
   (*a*) The long lines are not rhythm run to seed: everything is weighed and timed in them. Wait till they have taken hold of your ear and you will find it so.
   (*b*) I do not of course claim to have invented *sprung rhythms* but only *sprung rhythm:* I mean that single lines and single instances of it are not uncommon in English . . . *e.g.* 'why should this: desert be'? . . . 'There to meet: with Macbeth' or 'There to meet with Macbeth'; Campbell has some— 'and their fleet along the deep: proudly shone' and ... 'as ye sweep: through the deep,' etc.; in Nursery Rhymes, Weather Saws, and Refrains they are very common— but what I do in the *Deutschland,* etc., is to enfranchise them as a regular and permanent principle of scansion. [1877.]
   (*c*) Sprung rhythm, once you hear it, is so eminently natural a thing and so effective a thing that if they *[earlier poets*] had known of it they would have used it. Many people, as we say, have been 'burning' but they all-missed it; they took it up and mislaid it again. . . . In a matter like this a thing does not exist, is not *done* unless it is wittingly and willingly done; to recognise the form you are employing and to mean it is everything. [1882.]
5. Do the following quotations from Hopkins explain why the difficulty of grasping '*rove over,*' '*hangers* or *outrides*' is mainly one of the eye?—
   (*a*) The scanning runs on without break to the end of the stanza, so that each stanza is rather one long line rhymed in passage than four lines with rhymes at the ends.
   (*b*) Of this long Sonnet above all remember what applies to all my verse, that it is, as living art should be, made

for performance and that its performance is not reading with the eye but loud, leisurely, poetical (not rhetorical) recitation, with long rests, long dwells on the rhyme, and other marked syllables. [1886.]

6. Test the following note on Hopkins's alliteration by the examples given:

   The alliteration so largely present in his poems is significant. . . . It is of course a habit prevalent in all poets, but in general it is intentionally disguised; the inexpert reader will not easily believe how much of it is in Shakespeare. . . . The astonishing thing about Swinburne is not its presence but its uselessness, as the admirable thing about Hopkins is not its presence but its use. [C. Williams, Preface to Hopkins's *Poems,* 1930.]

7. Attempt an expansion of some of Hopkins's compound words on the lines of the following:—

   By *moon marks* I mean crescent-shaped markings on the quill-feathers, either in the colouring of the feather or made by the overlapping of one on another. [Sonnet, 'Henry Purcell'—"quaint moon marks, to his pelted plumage under Wings ..."

8. What similarity exists between Hopkins's aims and the following, Point 2 of the Principles of the Imagist movement?—

   To create new rhythms—-as the expression of new moods—and not to copy old rhythms, which merely echo old moods. We do not insist upon "free verse" as the only method of writing poetry. We fight for it as a principle of liberty. We believe that the individuality of a poet may often be better expressed in free verse than in conventional forms. In poetry a new cadence means a new idea.

9. Laurence Housman wrote the following to his brother:—

   What makes many of your poems more obscure than they need be is that you do not put yourself in the reader's place and consider how, and at what stage, that man of sorrows is to find out what it is all about. You are behind the scenes and know all the data; but he knows only what you tell him.

How much of this can be applied to (*a*) Hopkins; (*b*) all poets?

10. Estimate the value in this exposition of Hopkins's poetry of the following:—
    (*a*) The critic's strong sense of tradition.
    (*b*) His receptiveness—his ability to give new works in a new form a fair hearing.
    (*c*) His refusal to use other poets as ninepins, to be knocked down with malice or glee so that the favoured poet alone can be left standing.
    (*d*) His readiness to let the theorist speak for himself.
    (*e*) His generosity in quoting.
    (*f*) The order of the points he discusses.
    (*g*) The concentration on the subject—Hopkins, not Read.

XVII

1. Does Mr. Auden's classification of 'poets who live in the country' allow room for a man like Cowper, a man bred in the country but quite unable to do the manual labour of a farm, neither a land-worker nor a land-owner, but a land-lover?
2. Into which grouping would you put (*a*) Robert Burns; (*b*) W. H. Davies (author of *The Autobiography of a Super Tramp*); (*c*) Thomas Hardy?
3. To what points made by Mr. Auden does this correspond? Like Virgil, he has been a farmer; and this ensured that his nature-poetry should not degenerate into false romanticism, whimsicality, heartiness, or mere botanizing. It is also important that Frost is a highly civilized man. He feels nature deeply: but his emotion is always passed through a filter of ironic detachment before it emerges in his verse. [C. Day Lewis on Robert Frost.]
4. Is it likely that Mr. Frost (of whom Mr. Auden says, "He describes what he knows without comment") would be openly didactic?
5. What qualities or features of poetry does an intimacy with Nature, gained by the experience of work, (*a*) prevent, (*b*) encourage?
6. Give other examples of 'poetry about the country' that 'would be immediately understood and appreciated by countrymen.'
7. Suggest a third group of readers, in addition to 'townees' and 'countryman' (*i.e.* one earning a living on the land).
8. How do you think Mr. Auden would reply to these?—
   (*a*) The difference between cultured people and uncultured people, in regard to their response to Nature, is that the former make a lot of a little, whereas the latter make little of a lot. By this I mean that the less cultured you are, the more you require from Nature before you can be aroused to reciprocity. Uncultured people require

blazing sunsets, awe-inspiring mountains, astonishing waterfalls, masses of gorgeous flowers, portentous signs in the heavens, exceptional weather on earth, before their sensibility is stirred to a response. Cultured people are thrilled through and through by the shadow of a few waving grass blades upon a little flat stone, or by a single dock-leaf growing under the railings of some city square. [J. C. Powys.]

(*b*) What if it be true that scenic (or any other) beauty is the creation of the observer and does not exist as an absolute apart from his thoughts? . . . A field of corn, after all, is as utilitarian as a row of pylons. Is it only thinking that makes one a picture of loveliness and the other an outrageous incongruity? [Philip Tomlinson.]

9. Are these verses samples of "Nature Poetry"?

(*a*) Like shocks in a reaped field of rye
    The small black heaps of lively dung
Sprinkled in the grass-meadow lie
    Licking the air with smoky tongue.

(*b*) I saw some sheep upon some grass,
    The sheep were fat, the grass was green,
The sheep were white as clouds that pass,
    And greener grass was never seen;
I thought, "Oh, how my bliss is deep,
With such green grass and such fat sheep!"